Art Works

Drawings by Ken Woolley

Stephen and Yuana Hesketh are magnificent benefactors of the New England Regional Art Museum (NERAM). They live in the former Woolley House in Mosman and first suggested to me that an exhibition of Ken Woolley's non-architectural drawings would be ideal for an intimate showing in Armidale.

It was a privilege to meet Ken and view his 'deliberate drawings or sketches which interest [him] for one reason or another'. A rather urbane man who speaks softly, he nevertheless draws with an intent which presupposes strength and clarity. The drawings are distinctly his and present a body of work that has not been seen by more than a handful of people. It is now, in part, available to a wider audience both as an exhibition and as a book.

It is always a pleasure to see a project based on an exhibition come to fruition. In this case the drawings by Ken Woolley are no exception. Here now we have a small exhibition and book of a much larger man, Ken Woolley, a most distinguished Australian architect.

NERAM has pleasure in presenting both the exhibition and the book for you to enjoy.

Joseph Eisenberg, OAM
Director
New England Regional Art Museum

Contents

First published in Australia in 2002
by The Images Publishing Group Pty Ltd
ABN 89 059 734 431
6 Bastow Place, Mulgrave, Victoria, 3170, Australia
Telephone: +61 3 9561 5544
Facsimile: + 61 3 9561 4860
books@images.com.au
www.imagespublishinggroup.com

The Images Publishing Group Reference Number: 496

National Library of Australia
Cataloguing-in-Publication data
Woolley, Ken, 1933 –
Art works: the drawings of Ken Woolley

ISBN 1 876907 79 7

1. Woolley, Ken, 1933 – Exhibitions. I. Title

741.994

Designed by The Graphic Image Studio Pty Ltd

Film separations by Mission Productions Limited

Printed in China by Excel United Company Ltd

'Drawings of What I Can Draw'

Architect and Artist: An Exhibition of Work by Ken Woolley

Ken Woolley was born in Sydney in 1933 and studied architecture at the University of Sydney where he graduated with honours. In 1955 he won the prestigious University medal. In 1964 Woolley became a partner in the firm Ancher Mortlock Murray & Woolley, which was founded by Sydney Ancher in 1945. Prior to this, Woolley's considerable architectural experience was gained during nine years as design architect with the soberly named Government Architect's Branch of the NSW Public Works Department. While the title of this position alone conjures up visions of a kind of nineteenth-century utilitarianism, it was a period nevertheless when Woolley honed and disciplined his skills. The constraints inherent in working within the Public Works Department did not lessen Woolley's determination (and some might argue his inability) to divorce art from architecture. Architecture, 'wherever it is practised', says Woolley, 'must be practised like an art. To do otherwise [reduces the architect] to simply an arranger of buildings'.

While Woolley's impressive civic buildings are a public avowal of this philosophy, the architect's travel drawings, made over several decades, offer a window into the private expression of his belief relating to the indivisibility of architecture and art. All were a result of the artist's compulsion to record the architecture, the people and, to a lesser extent, the costume and landscapes of the world around him. As Woolley himself admits, he seldom draws landscape, vegetation, 'dress' or even people for their own sake, but rather as an attempt to understand and record the built environment.

These drawings have given Woolley, and now the viewer, a gentle pleasure in both their rendering and appreciation. Most of the drawings were completed in foreign lands as the artist stood on a busy corner, or in early or late moments that found him gazing and sketching from hotel windows.

Windows have provided a fruitful starting point for many of these works. 'Windows', quipped Woolley in an interview for this essay are, after all, an 'architectural sort of thing'. They provide 'some kind of containing structure and organisation', but do not act as a starting point for the works, even in those where a view framed by a window provides the most apparent optical device. A series of 'simple dots on the page' is used, according to Woolley, to indicate where each drawing will start and finish. These dots operate only as a starting point. Then comes an unselfconscious completion of the work that is sometimes halted only by 'running out of paper'.

The images, spanning almost 50 years and almost as many places, are fresh, unlaboured and notable for their economy of line. Woolley admits that the most successful of these sketches have been executed rapidly with most of the works completed in under an hour. Several works reveal Woolley's long and passionate affair with perspective. (The artist had some notoriety as a perspectivist in his early years at Sydney University). The eye is, of course, drawn by the careful use of perspective in many of these works, but other sketches employ Woolley's unselfconscious desire (inspired in part by Brett Whiteley's earnest entreaty) to 'distort, distort, distort!'. Although many of the sketches presented here honour the architect's reverence of perspective, and simultaneously entertain Whiteley's dictum to distort, they do nonetheless also honour a 'truth' that cannot be located without a direct reference to reality. And herein lies their primary charm.

The sketches are at once recognisable impressions and a realistic catalogue of adventures in lands that are unquestionably 'other'. They operate, much like sketches from a Victorian 'grand tour' travel diary might, to record an appreciative traveller's gaze, and are characterised by an affection that is perhaps unattainable by camera. Woolley does use a camera, is a skilled photographer and, as an interesting aside, knew Max Dupain *very well*, but a camera was never employed to create these works - all were drawn on site and capture the moment as a result. Although Woolley also uses photography to record his travels, he never photographs and sketches the same subject. The camera and the pen are tools with clearly delineated functions and intents.

Interestingly, Woolley has developed his pen techniques over the last few years, in part because of his (self-perceived) inability to paint in oils. He learnt painting techniques from the age of 11 at East Sydney Art School and, despite being encouraged and taught by Lloyd Rees and Roland Wakelin when at Sydney University, Woolley insists that he was no good at oils and only a little better with watercolour and hasn't touched either since he was 21. Pen techniques offered, according to Woolley and somewhat modestly, 'a tiny, narrow, niche that I could do as well as anyone'.

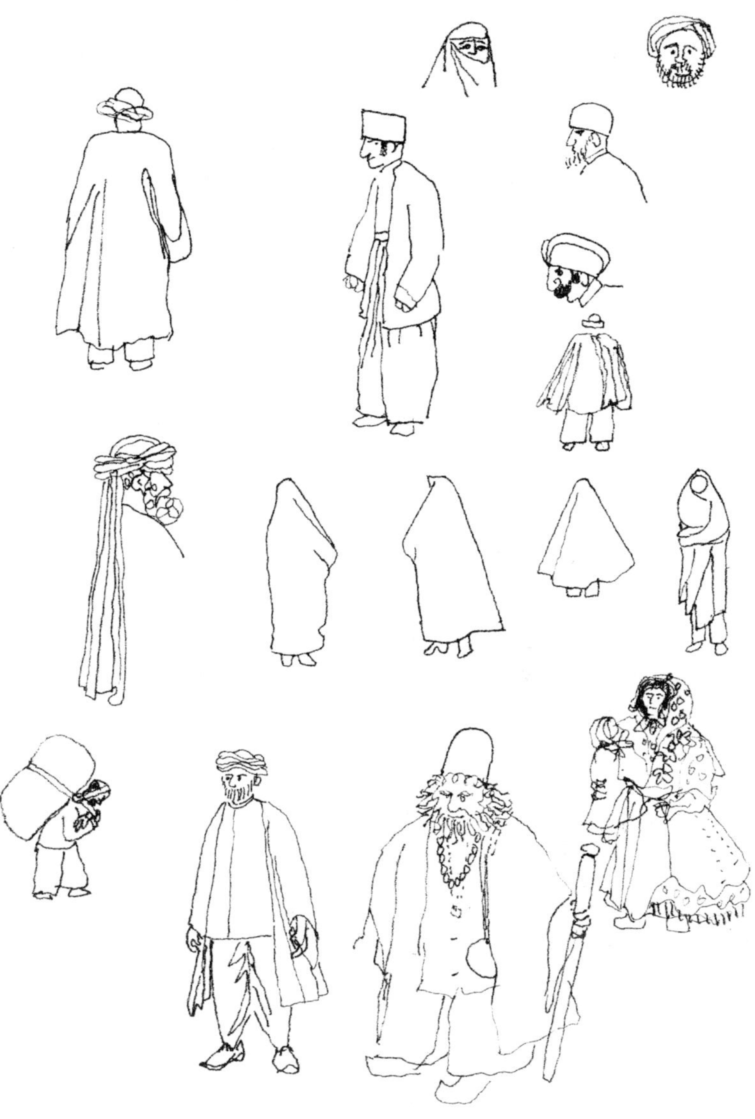

Iranians 1977

Pilot Fineliner, cartridge paper 11.5 x 17 Exhibited

Despite his reluctance to paint, Woolley prefers to use a fibre pen, specifically because its results are more like a brush than a nib. He developed a 'brush' technique over the years using the pen as a calligrapher might. He remembers with candour the limitations of pens, nibs and inks that were available in the 1950s. Woolley cared little for pencil as an art medium (seeing it as too light) and struggled with the technology of fountain pens of that era. The best results were obtained by using a piston-action pen in which the kerosene-based ink was poured in at one end, while marks were made by the clumsy, brush-like device at the other. Technological advances, particularly in the Pentel pens in the 1960s, made his sketches easier to complete, but by that time the demands of his promising architectural career, combined with the responsibilities of raising a young family, left little time for sketching.

As Woolley admits, he has never travelled to a particular destination with the intention of drawing it. Rather, the works are a response to 'accidental circumstances, and they may or may not coincide with [his] concerns about a place'. They are, he notes finally, simply 'drawings of what I can draw'. Viewers of this exhibition will, of course, recognise his talent, and be grateful for whatever took the artist, the architect and traveller to these, and distant shores.

Dr Leigh Summers, Curator/Education Officer
New England Regional Art Museum
Armidale, New South Wales, Australia

Ken Woolley: On Drawing

My early drawings were influenced by the traditions in architectural drawing represented at Sydney University, where I studied from 1950 to 1954, and particularly by Lloyd Rees who taught us art. A contrasting influence was George Molnar, our design tutor, who was then just getting into cartoon work for *The Sydney Morning Herald*. Rees' early drawings were in very finely detailed pencil, but it was very evident to his students that they freed up enormously when he was in Europe in 1953. Molnar, on the other hand, used sparse linework and filled chosen areas very graphically in solid black. Alan Gamble was also teaching architecture in the faculty at the time, and doing his marvellous traditional pen drawings of Sydney buildings. Therefore, I was influenced by an abundance of different styles.

Earlier, I had studied at junior classes at East Sydney Art School, mostly painting in gouache and drawing in pencil. My mother was a fine draftsman and encouraged me from an early age. My father was a printer, involved at one time in art reproduction in the laborious multi-colour processes of the day, perhaps imbuing me with the need to be patient and meticulous.

The architecture presentation drawings were in pencil with water colour and poster colour (gouache). Later, I supplemented my income doing architectural perspectives.

I started drawing places seriously while living in Europe for 18 months in 1956 on a scholarship. The early drawings were on the same Wire-O cartridge paper sketchbooks that Rees used and were seen in the recent exhibition of his work.

In the late 60s and early 70s I started drawing places again as a recreation. The Pentel pen opened up a new opportunity, working on heavy textured Ingres paper, to produce strong, black, graphic sketches with a wide range of line. The Pilot Fineliner suited the transfer of my thought process to miniature drawings in workbooks and the collection of little notes and observations that came with the opportunity to travel more frequently, particularly in Asia, when I started work on the Embassy in Bangkok in 1973.

Unfortunately the Pentel product became somewhat coarser in the 80s, reducing the range of expression, but I haven't found anything better.

I never go to a place in order to do drawings. I am there either for business, to look at some special buildings or as part of a study of places from an urban design point of view.

When there is an opportunity and I have a half-hour or so, I do a drawing if something interests me – usually it is about the place as a built environment.

Although I experimented with coloured pencil, I've rather lost interest in it. It does provide another dimension but is very different to the technique that seems to have served me best in most circumstances and in which I could possibly be a bit more original. With the Pentel, everything you do is visible. Spontaneity is essential, which suits limited time. Colour has to be done in layers and involves deliberate balancing of tone, light and shade and is less spontaneous. The black drawings impose conventions of line and black fill or hatching, which give an impression of light and space.

Because I usually draw when the time presents itself, it is often from hotel windows and balconies – opening up viewpoints along rooftops and down into space. I love drawing from terraces in towns. When I was younger I could draw standing, the pad without firm support, which allowed a number of interesting viewpoints, but now I often carry a folding stool. The viewpoint is critical. With few exceptions the drawings are views of places but some are notes on people or clothing, common objects and vegetation. As pictures of places they are fundamentally selective –of the view that describes the place, but also selective of what is shown. You can only show what can be depicted by the medium you are using, but you should also only show what is relevant.

Both photos and drawings are of what you find. You find if you seek. 'We are born seeing, but we still have to look.' (Goethe)

It is wrong to think of drawing as a substitute for photography. I am a keen photographer and think I have an eye for it, particularly for architecture and details. It is just a different matter than drawing. A drawing can take an hour, a photo an instant. A photo is often about an instant – the critical moment referred to by Cartier-Bresson. It can also be very deliberate, carefully considered and waited upon, to catch light or an event, but it is still an instant in time.

Many things that make good photos are unsuitable for drawings even though, with some trouble, a drawn record can be made of them. I don't think either photos or drawings should be merely records; they are both something taken, seized, appropriated for a purpose – which is to produce a two-dimensional artefact that gives pleasure and interest.

Wit, observation, comment and a demonstration of humanity should be present; they are not for mere decoration.

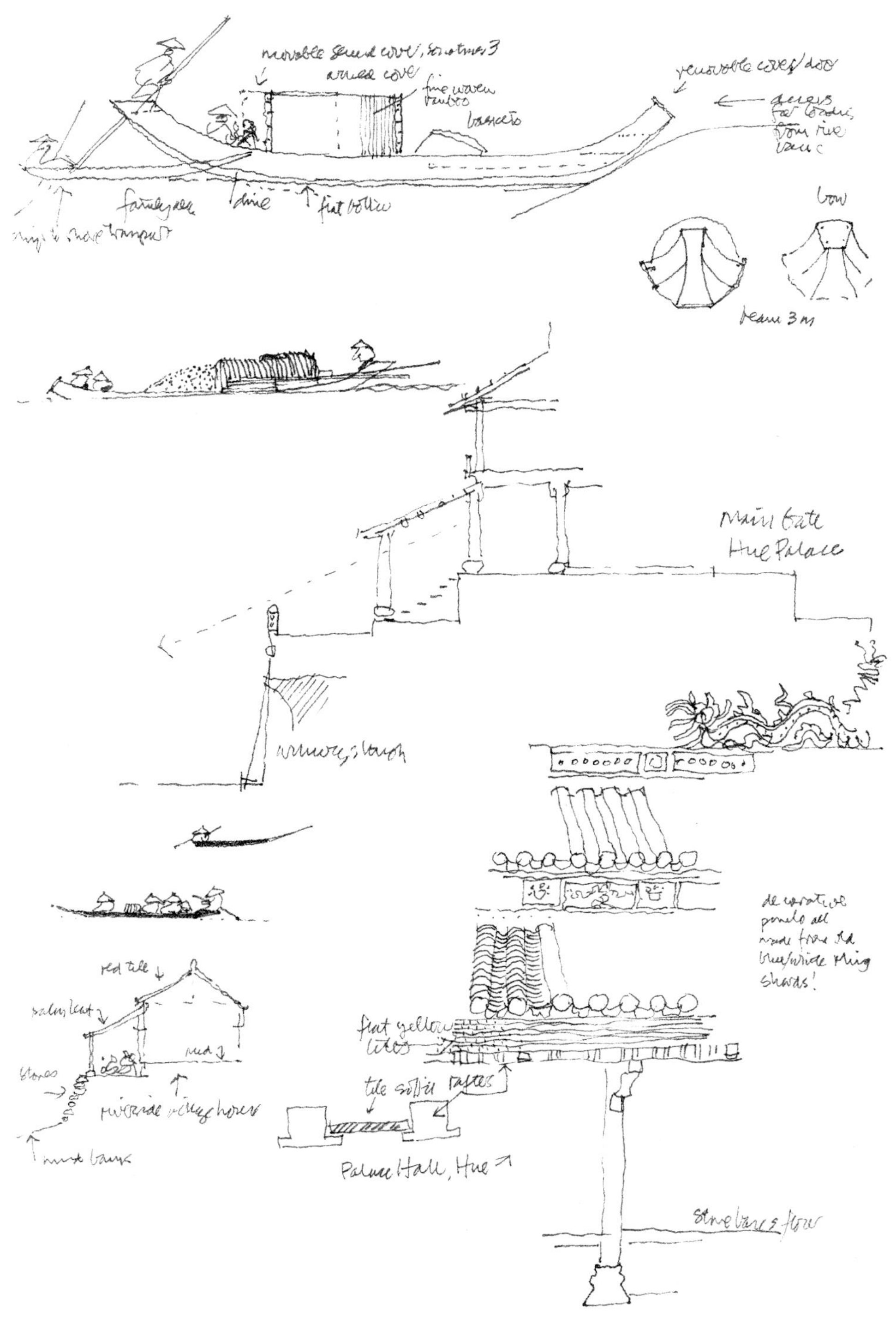

Notes in Hue, Vietnam 1994

Pilot Fineliner, Strathmore workbook, recycled paper 13 x 21.5

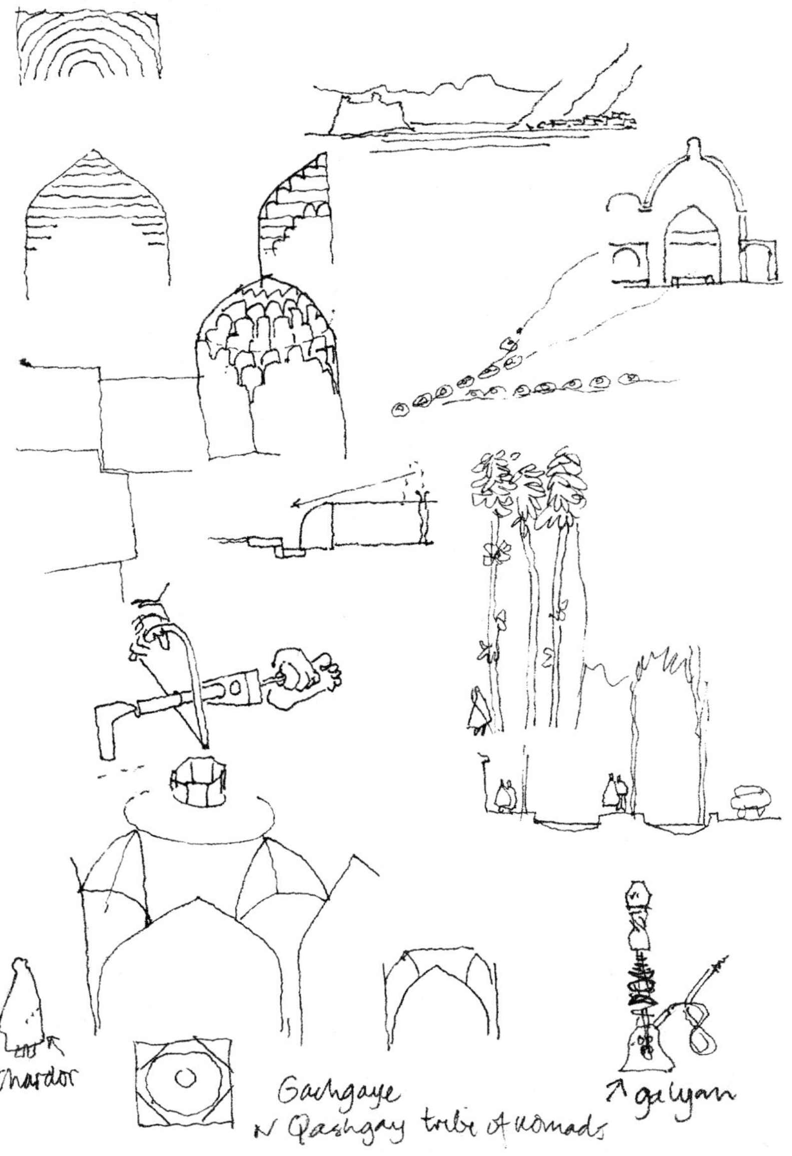

Notes in Iran

Ken Woolley: Drawing and Seeing

Ken Woolley likes to draw. He draws with apparent ease and style the large scale natural and urban landscape, buildings of architectural merit or of significant character and the vernacular; profile, surface and detail. He draws what he sees in distant lands, at home in Australia and in the office. And he sees a lot.

In a limited edition booklet of his sketches published to celebrate his fiftieth birthday, is a sketch from a window in Moscow. Here he annotates the character of the city, the texture of the historic wall and dome construction; and the detail of the modern hotel. It is an episodic drawing composing complete symmetrical elements with others shown incomplete, framed and kept in balance as a whole.

This way of seeing many levels or conditions of a place is a consistent trait of Woolley's drawings and exhibits his keen interest in all matters of architecture, and of the large scale environment. An important aspect of this travel and drawing is the appreciation and understanding that Woolley has for locally derived architecture: he recognises the necessity to build differently in differing climates and terrains, differing social and economic conditions, and differing points in time. And he recognises the recurring patterns in an environment seen up close, those elements and vernacular types which often are the most telling yet least observed because of their ubiquitous nature. Through the act of drawing he learns, because he takes time to study and know his subject.

This desire to know is extended to know well the places in which he works, and is supported by other forms of seeing. Of Sydney, his home and workplace, he knows the intimate historic relationships between building types and immediate locale, forms and geography, materials and fire laws, details and craftsmanship. He knows the regional and local climatic conditions and the varied plant life. And he knows too that the patterns and textures at the scale of the street are a result of economic patterns of activity and investment over time.

Harold Guida
Canberra, April 1985
Australian Architects: Ken Woolley
Royal Australian Institute of Architects, Sydney, 1985, p. 103

Ken Woolley AM

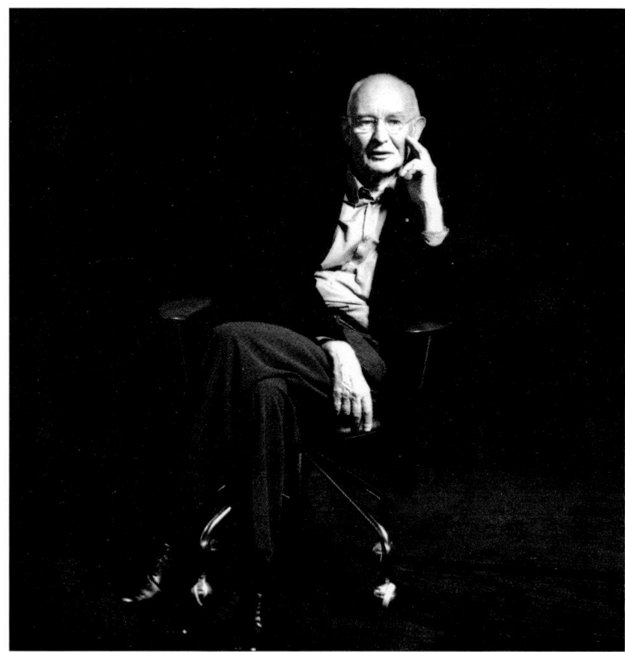

Photo credit: Bart Maiorana

Ken Woolley's buildings have received all the major architecture awards and range from low-cost production houses to large public buildings. Recent works include the Showground Dome and Hockey Stadium for the Sydney 2000 Olympic Games, the Control Tower at Sydney Airport, The Park Hyatt hotel at Circular Quay and the State Library of Victoria.

He became a Member of the Order of Australia in 1988 and was awarded the Gold Medal of the Royal Australian Institute of Architects in 1993.

His travel and notebook drawings have been exhibited and published in a 1983 private edition, an RAIA monograph in 1985 and an RAIA exhibition in 1984.
He was also the subject of a 1999 Images Publishing Group monograph, as part of its Master Architects Series.

The 32 drawings selected for exhibition at the New England Regional Art Museum in September 2002 are identified in the captions.

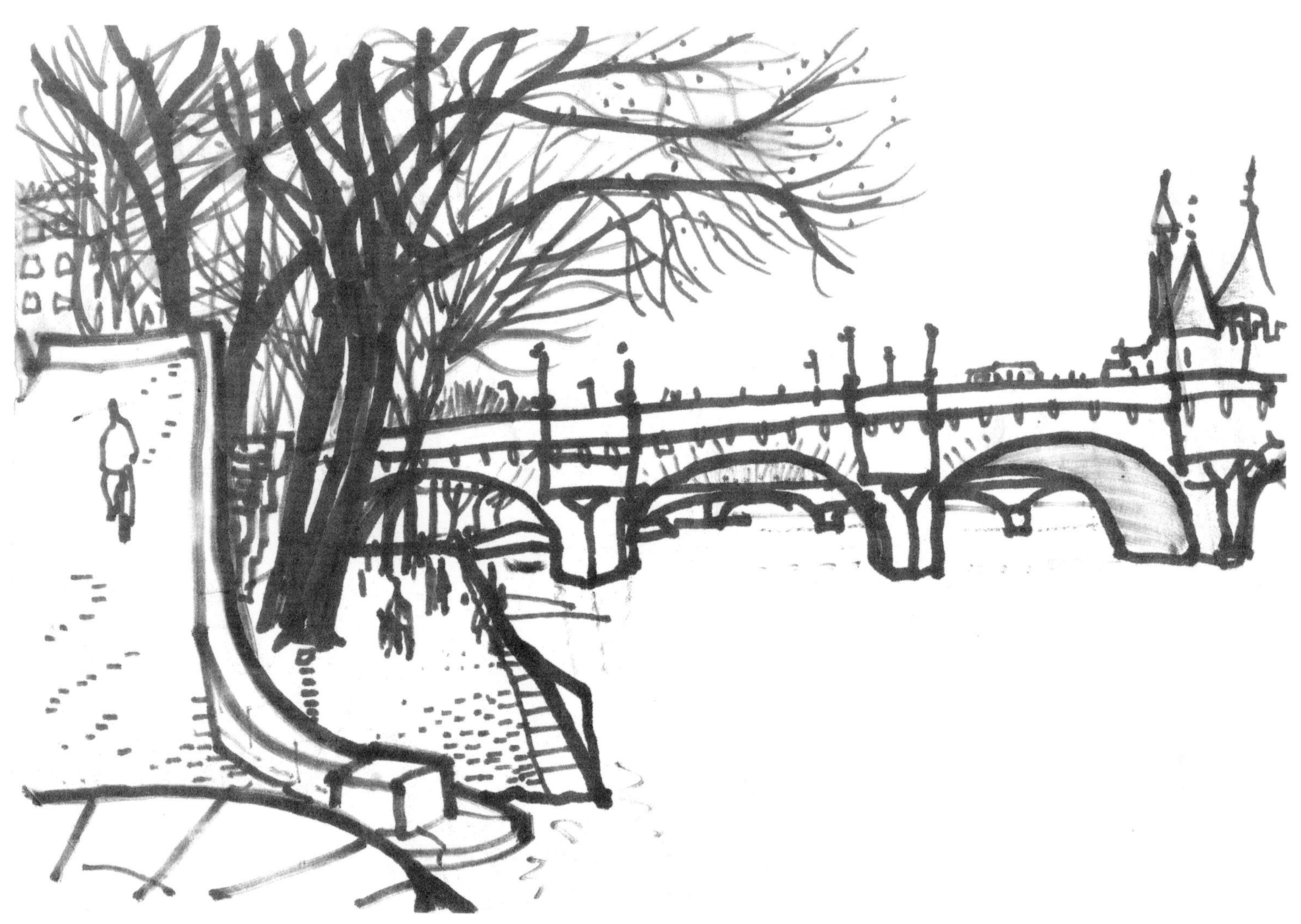

1

Seine embankment, Pont Neuf, Paris 1956

Felt and ink pen, cartridge Wire-O pad 14 x 19.5

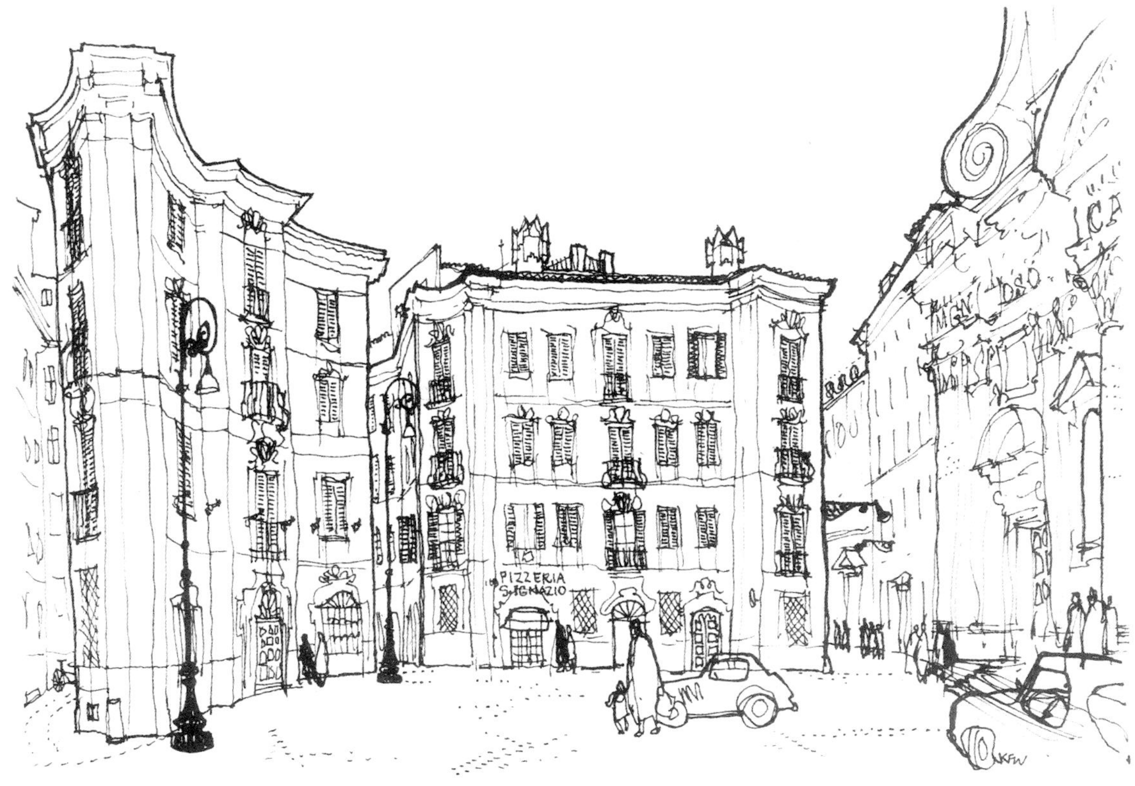

2

Piazza S. Ignazio, Rome 1956

Fountain pen, Indian ink, cartridge Wire-O pad 14 x 19.5

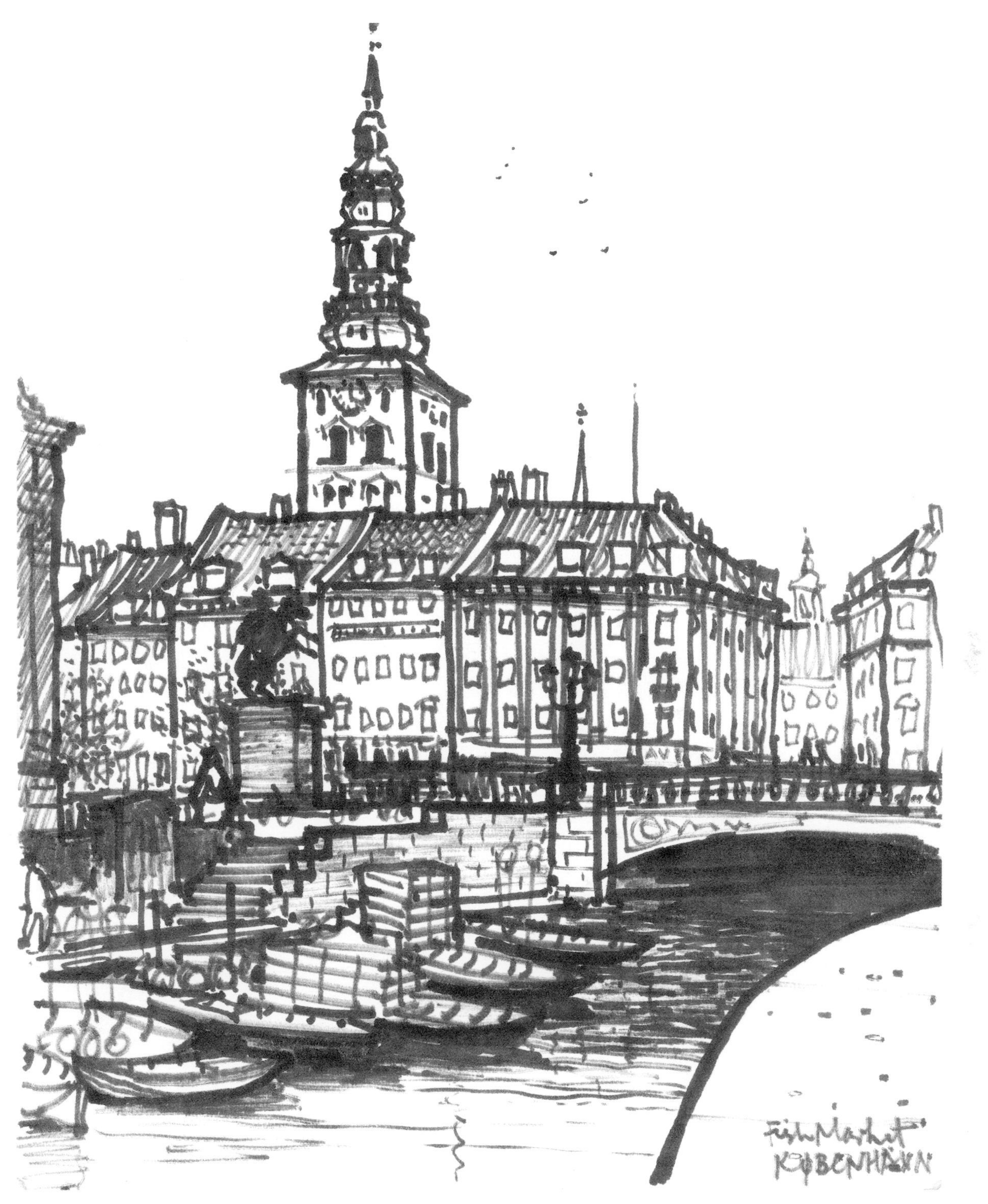

3

Fish Market, Copenhagen 1956

Felt and ink pen, cartridge paper 18 x 23 Exhibited

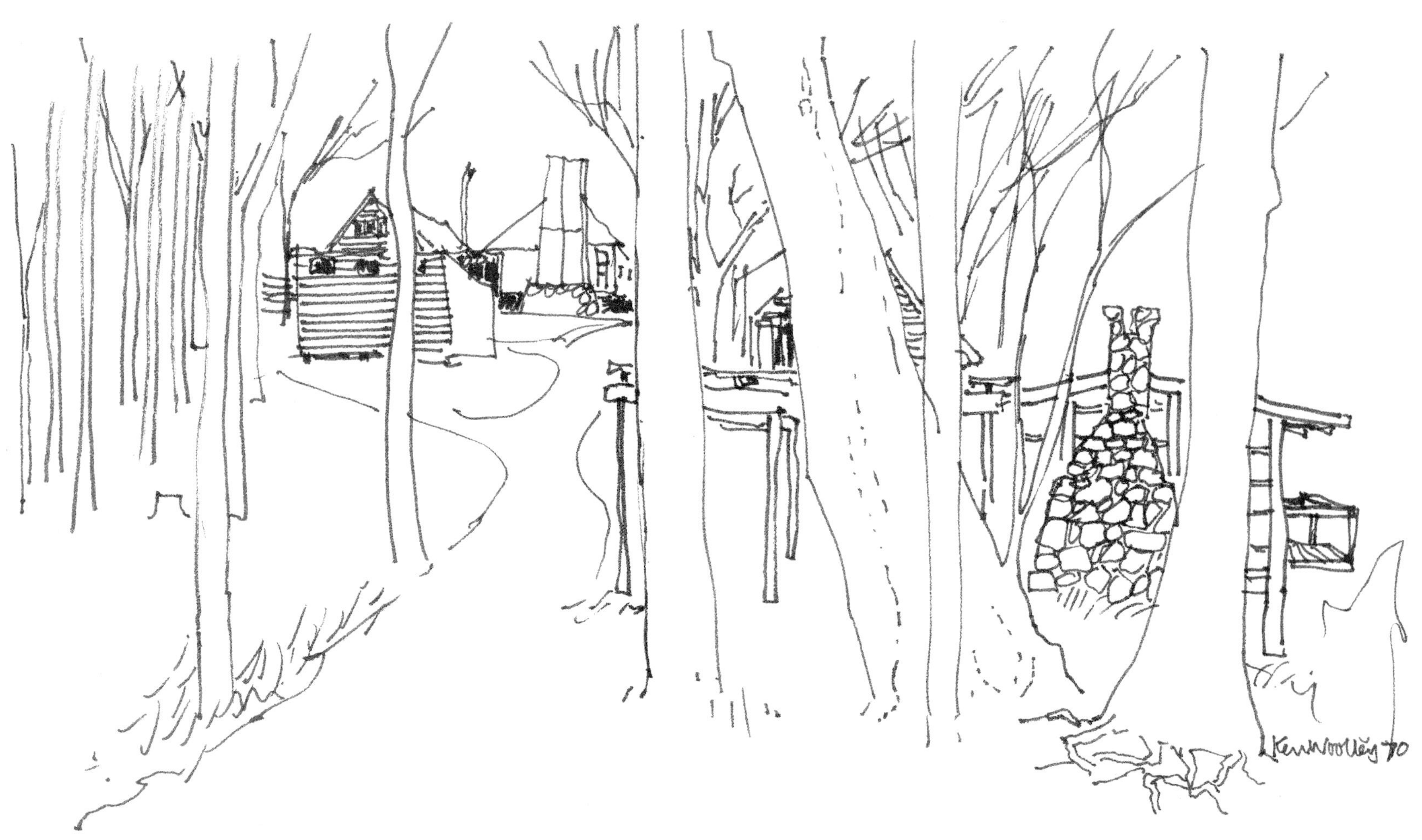

4

Binnaburra Lodge, Lamington National Park, Queensland 1970

Pentel, bond paper 17.5 x 26

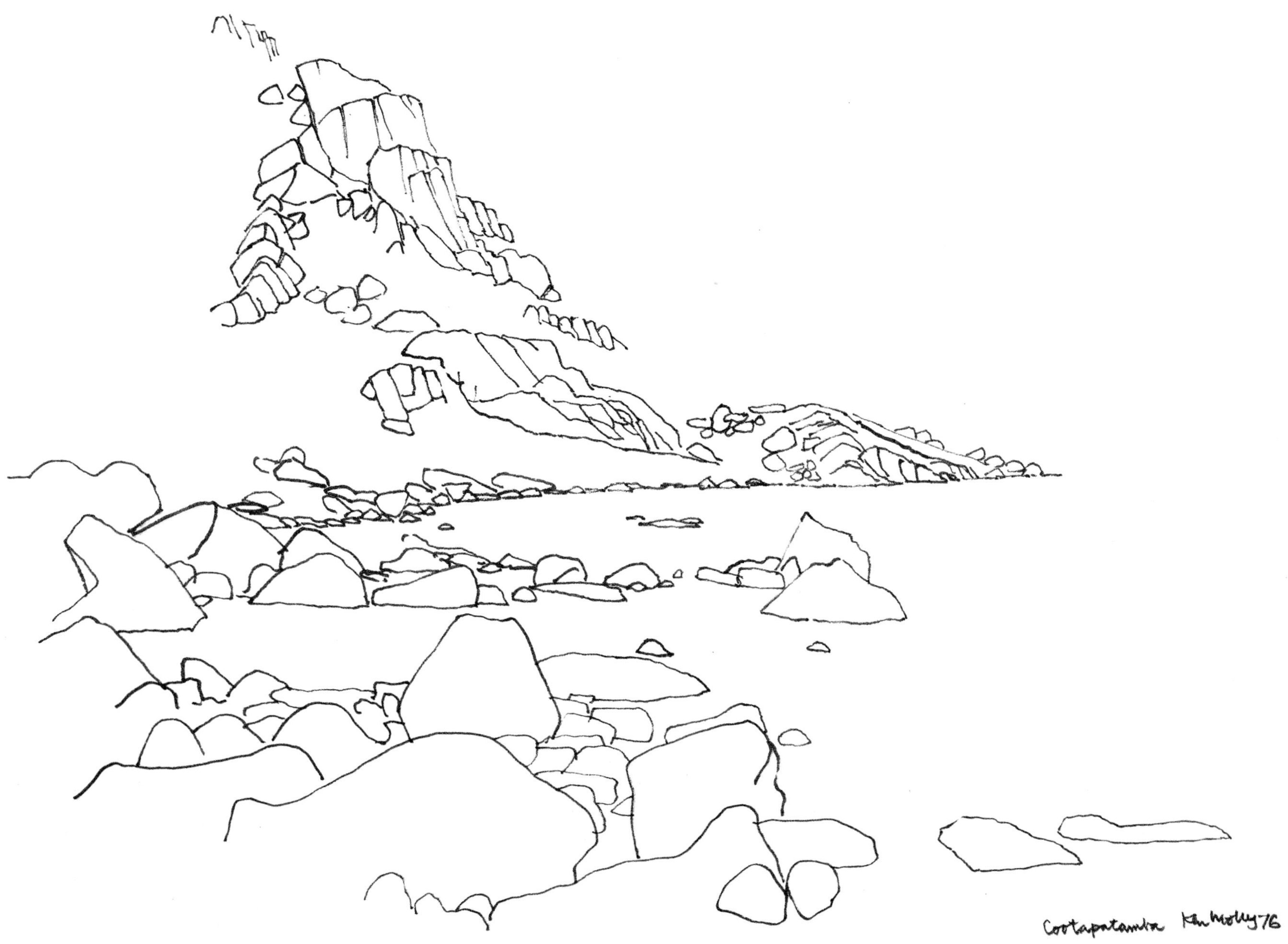

5

Lake Cootapatamba, Snowy Mountains, New South Wales 1976

Marker pen, cartridge paper 30 x 42

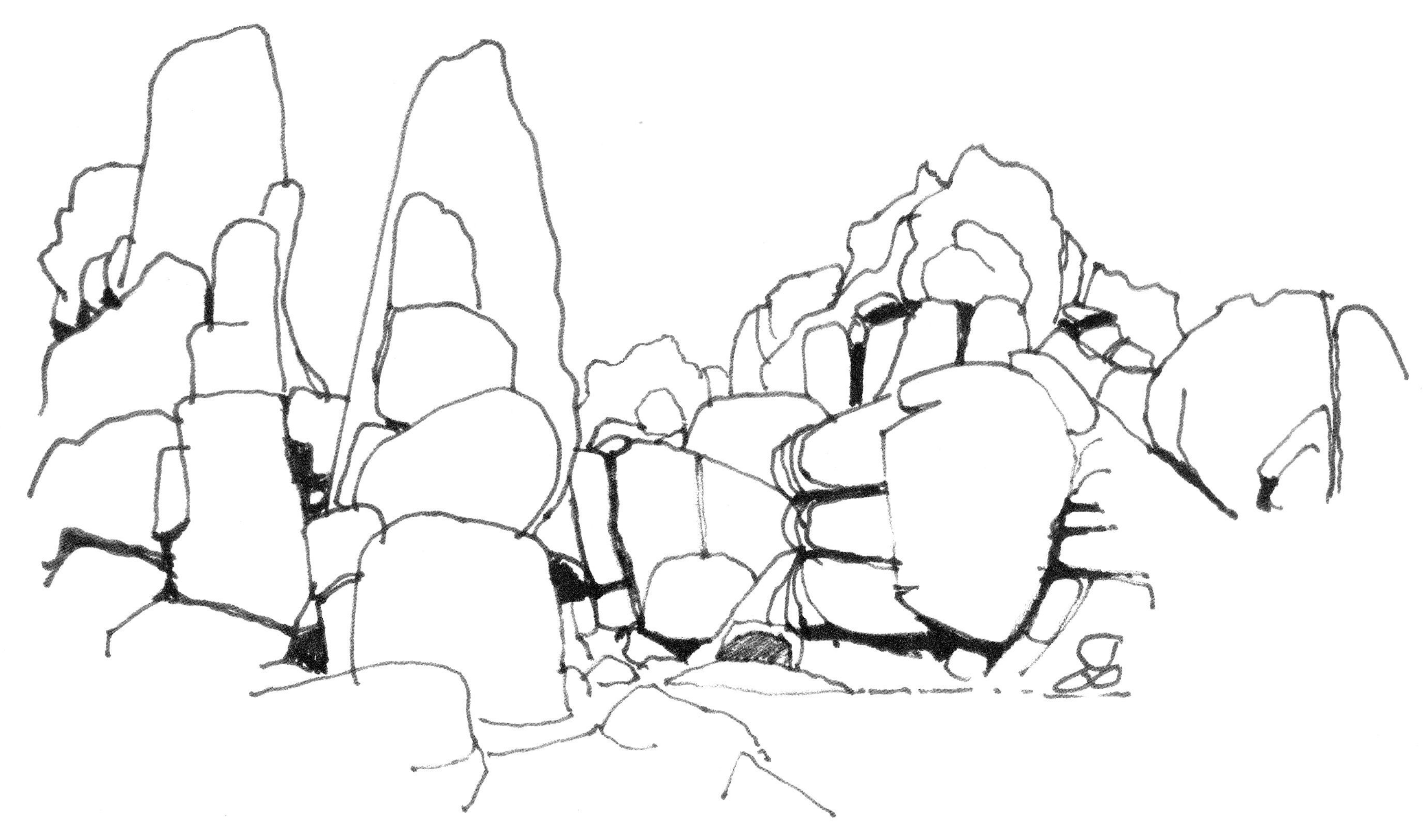

6

Ramshead Range, Snowy Mountains, New South Wales 1976

Marker pen, cartridge paper 34.5 x 18.5

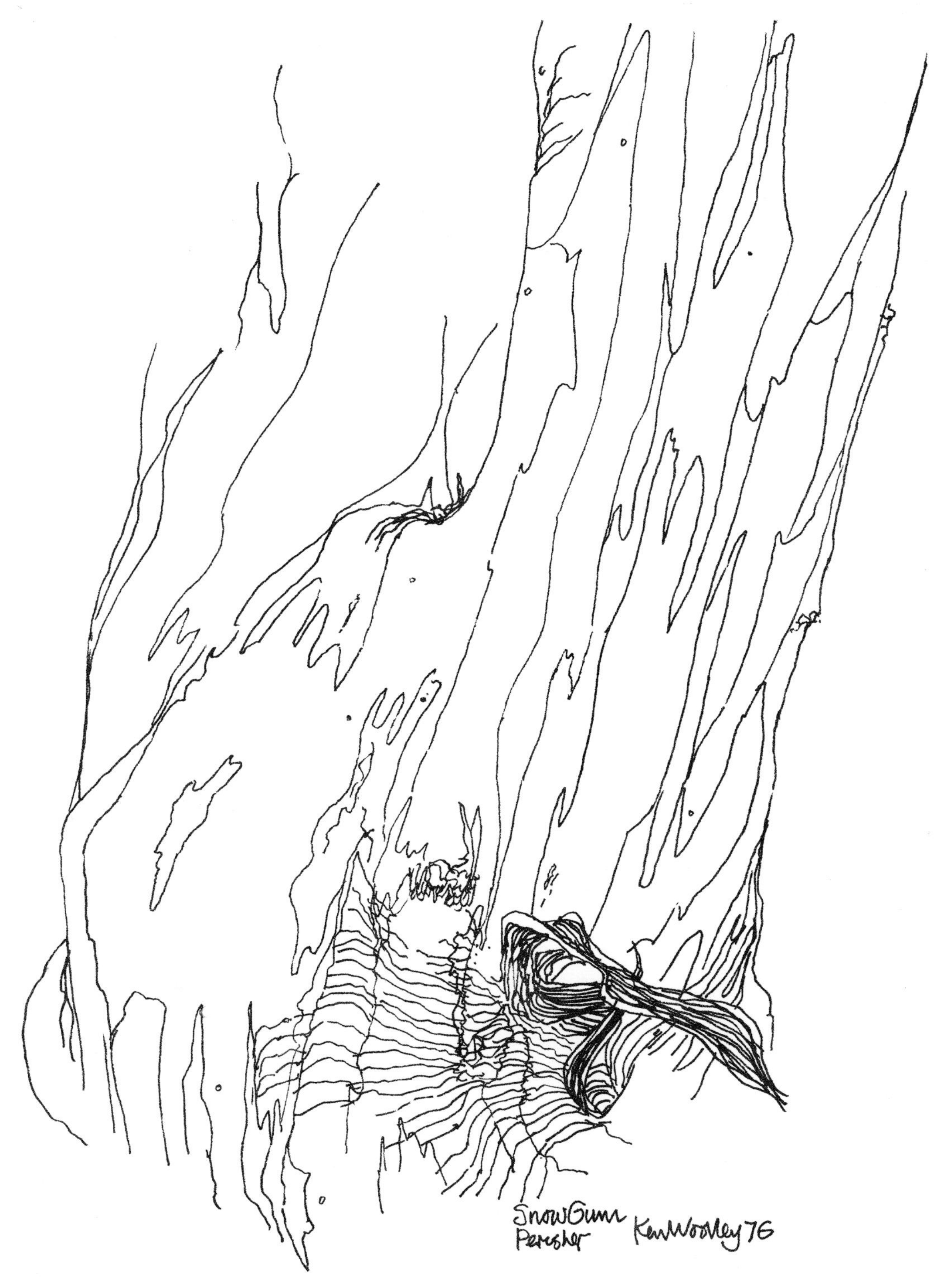

7

Snow Gum, Perisher Valley, New South Wales 1976

Pentel, cartridge paper 17.5 x 24

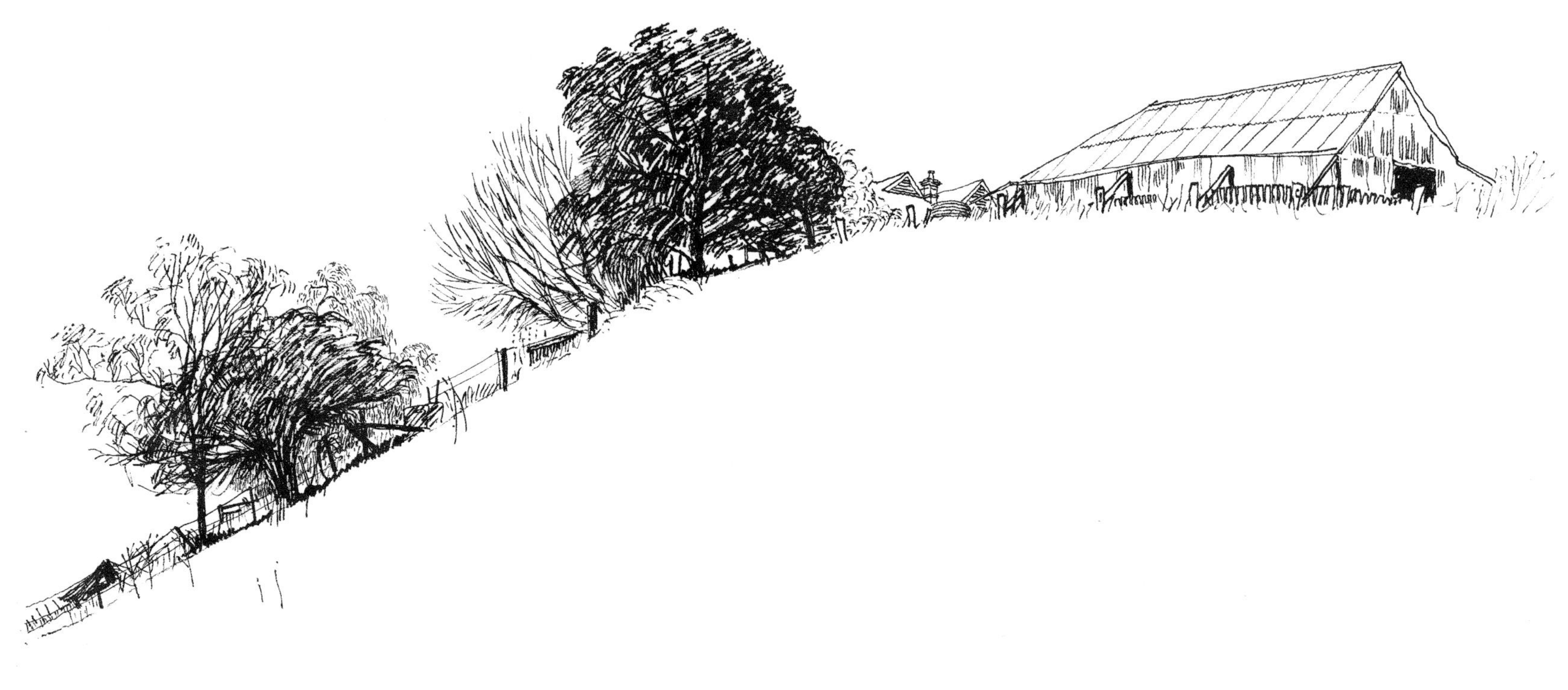

8

Farm Buildings, Mt. View, Hunter Valley, New South Wales 1976

Pentel, cartridge paper 30 x 42 Exhibited

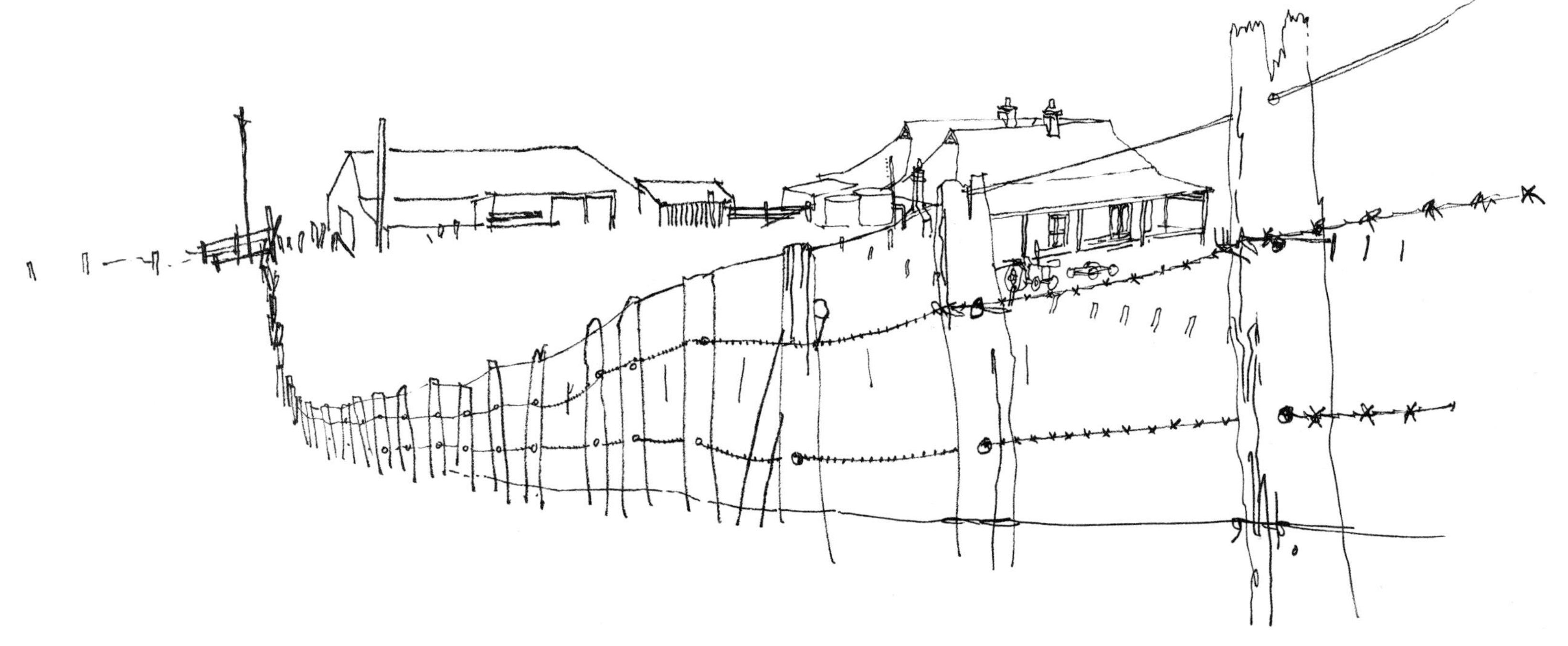

Mt View, Hunter Valley
Ken Woolley 76

9

Farm Buildings, Mt. View, Hunter Valley, New South Wales 1976

Pentel, cartridge paper 30 x 42 Exhibited

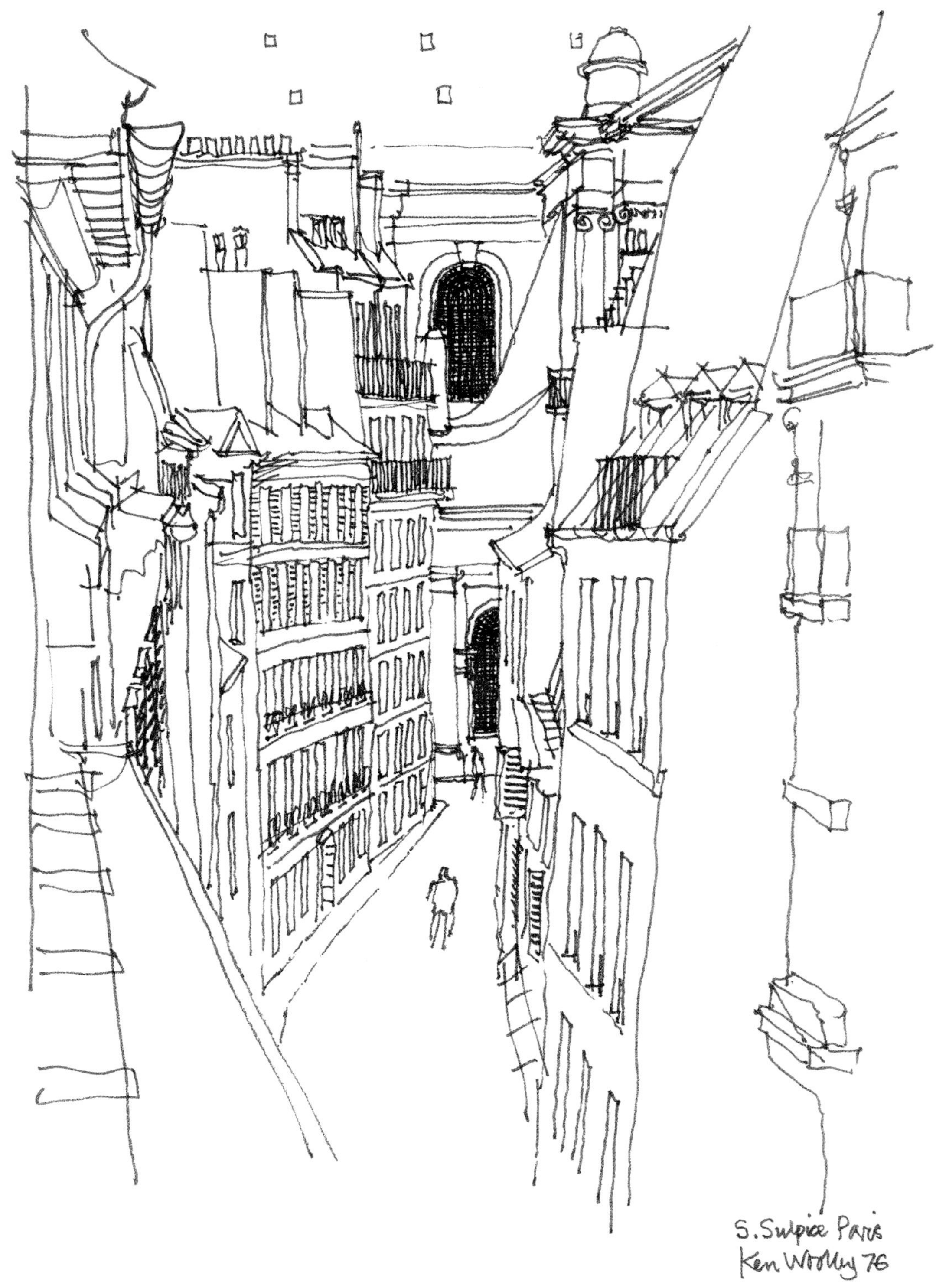

10
S. Sulpice, Paris 1976
Pentel, cartridge paper 17.5 x 24.5

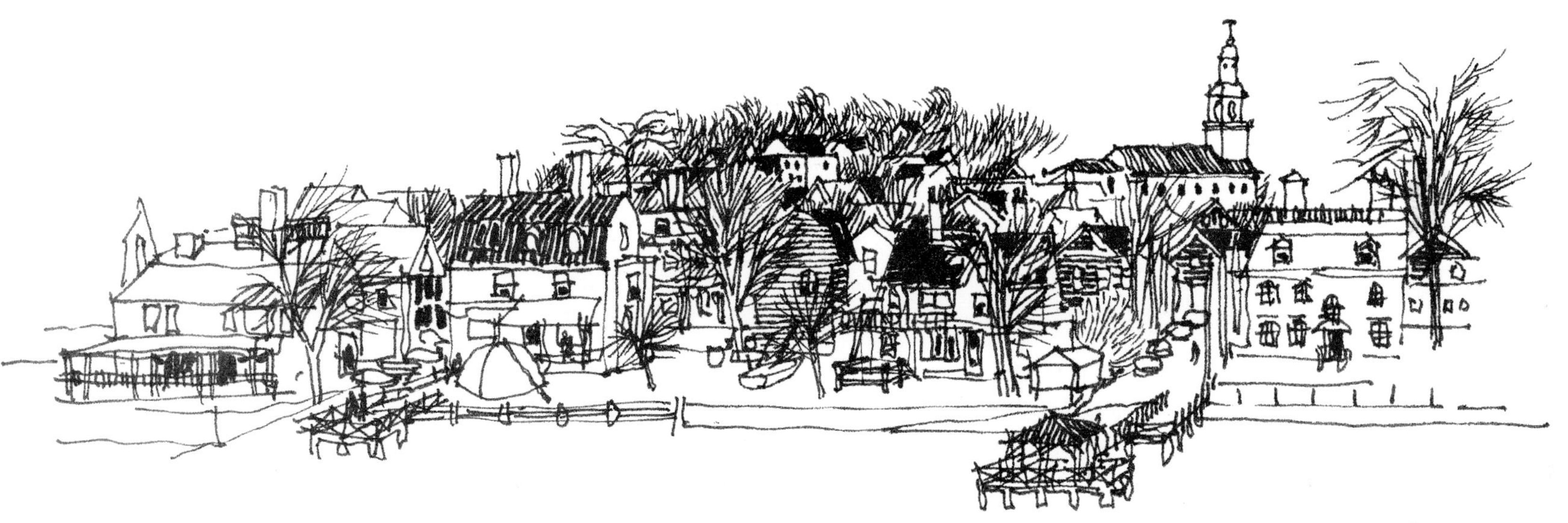

Newport R.I.
Ken Woolley 76

11

Newport, Rhode Island, USA 1976

Pentel, cartridge paper 17.5 x 24.5

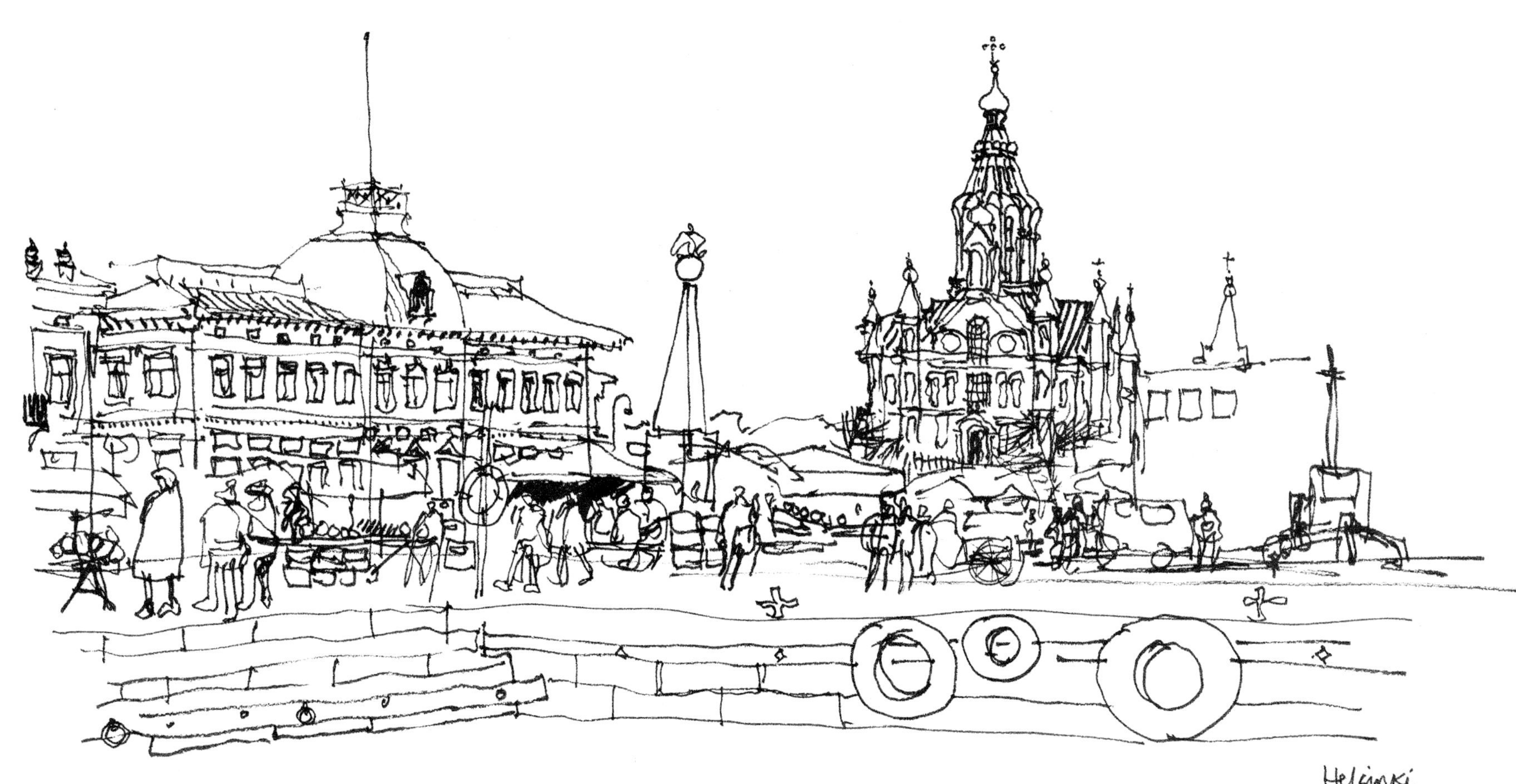

12

Waterfront Market, Ice, Helsinki 1976

Pentel, cartridge paper 17.5 x 24.5

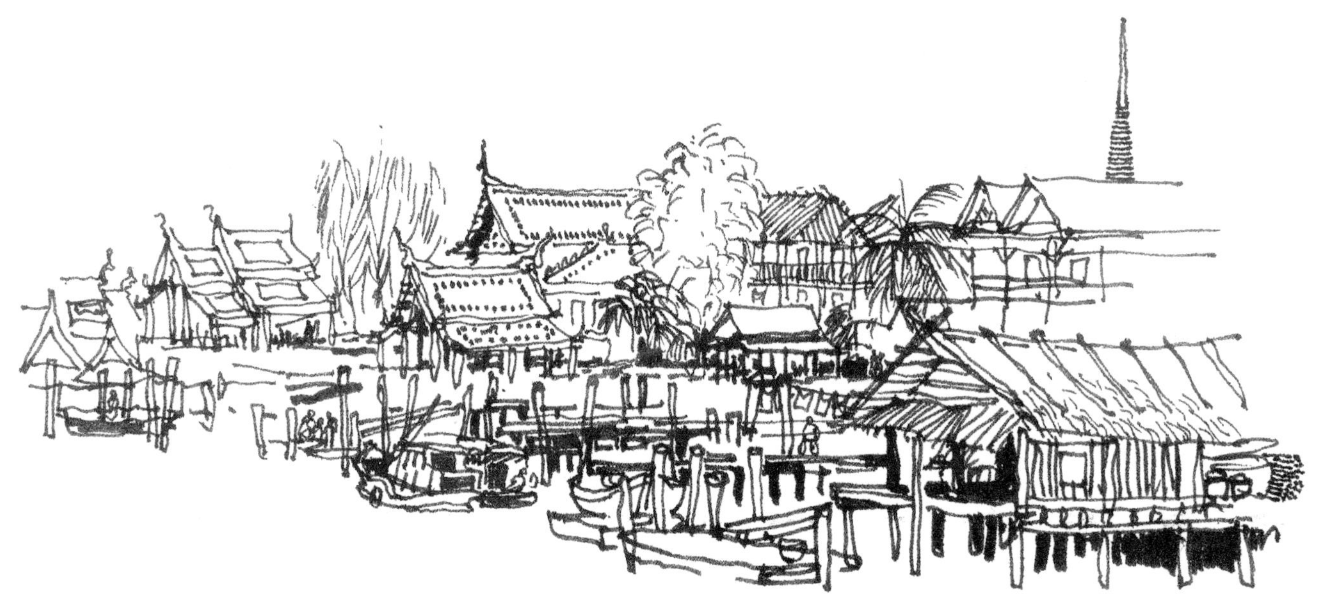

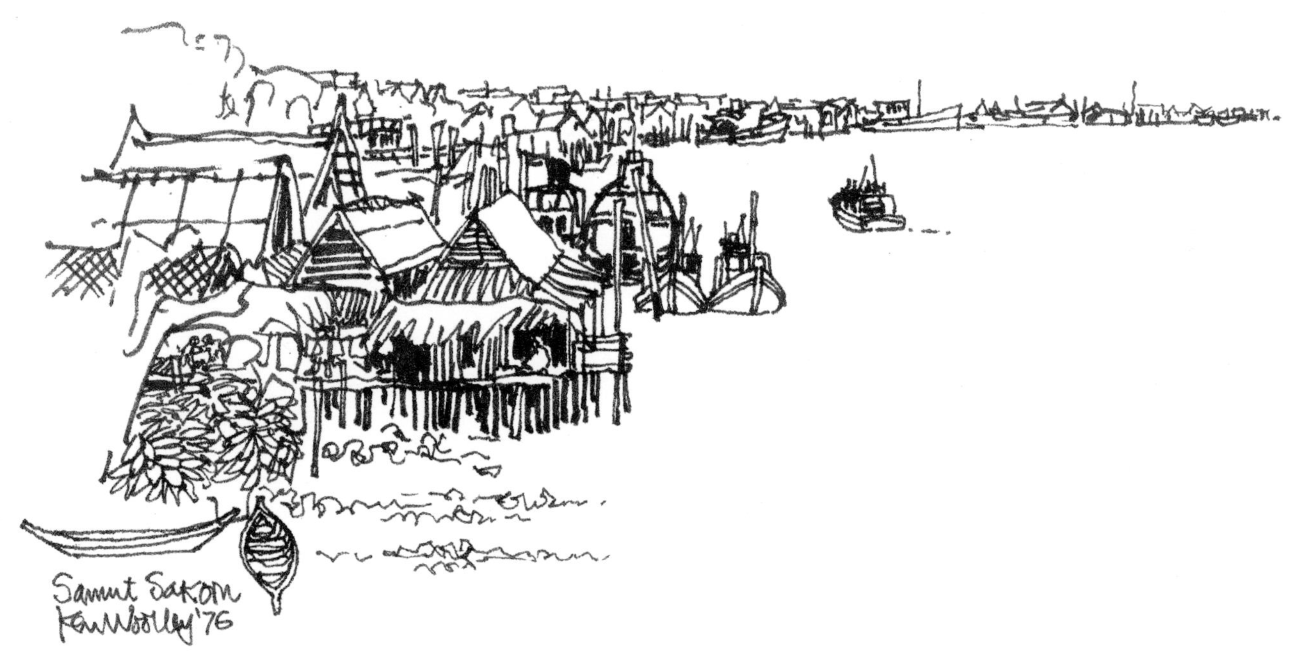

13 & 14
Sammut Sakorn, Thailand 1976
Pentel, cartridge paper 11.5 x 17

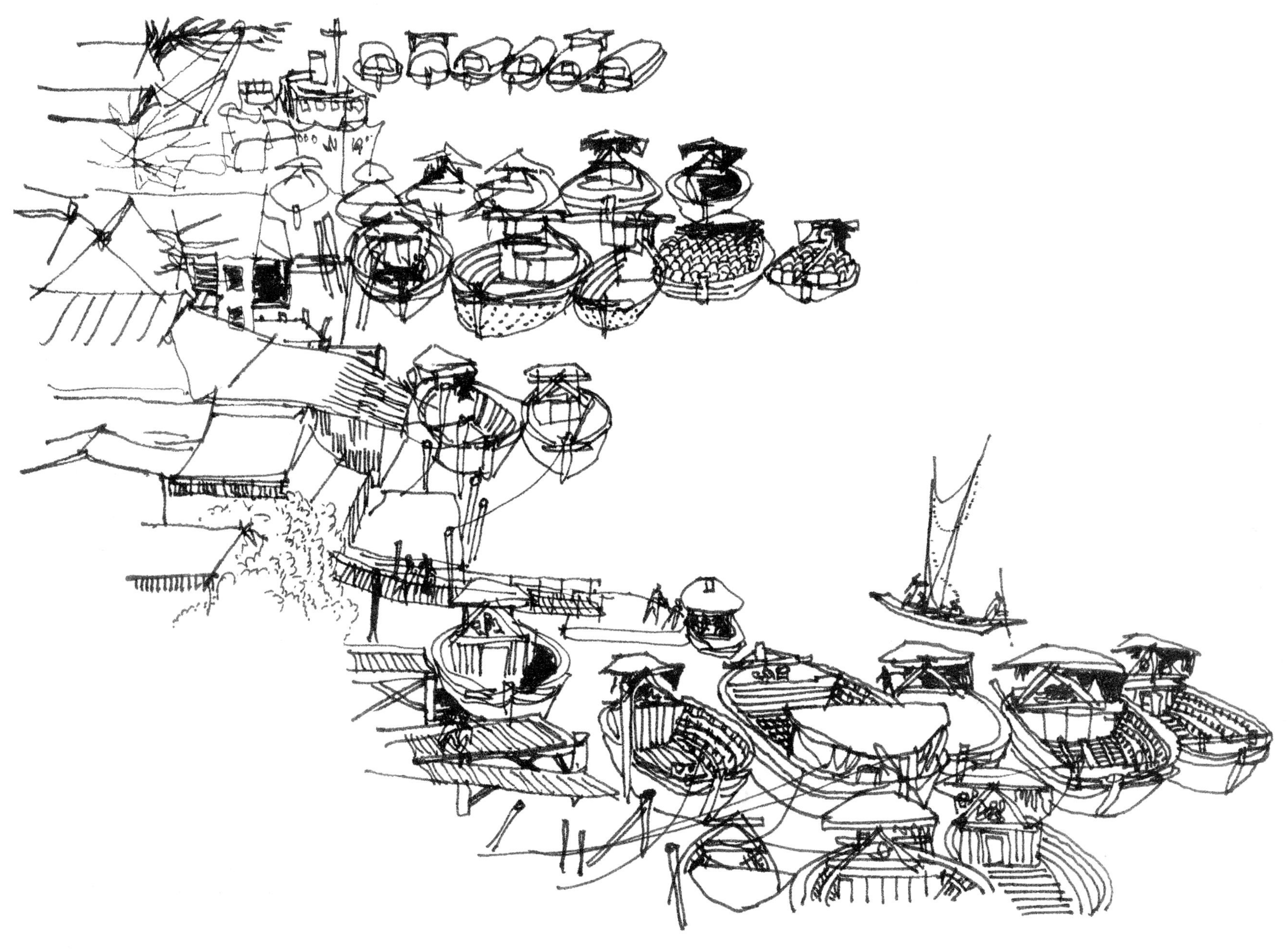

15
Rice barges on the Chao Praya, Bangkok 1976
Pentel, cartridge paper 17.5 x 24.5 Exhibited

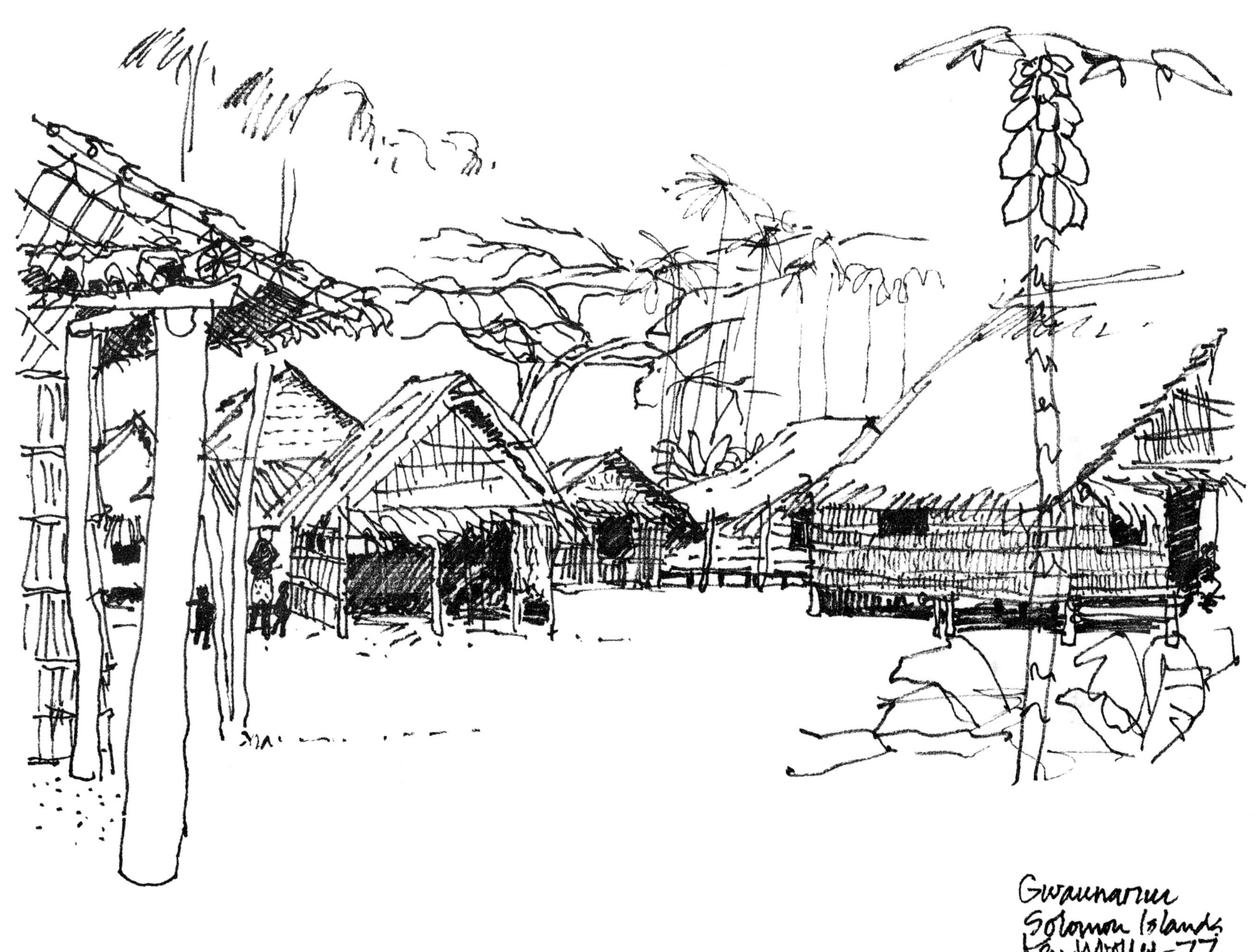

16

Gwaunarwa, Solomon Islands 1977

Pentel, Ingres paper 23.5 x 29.5

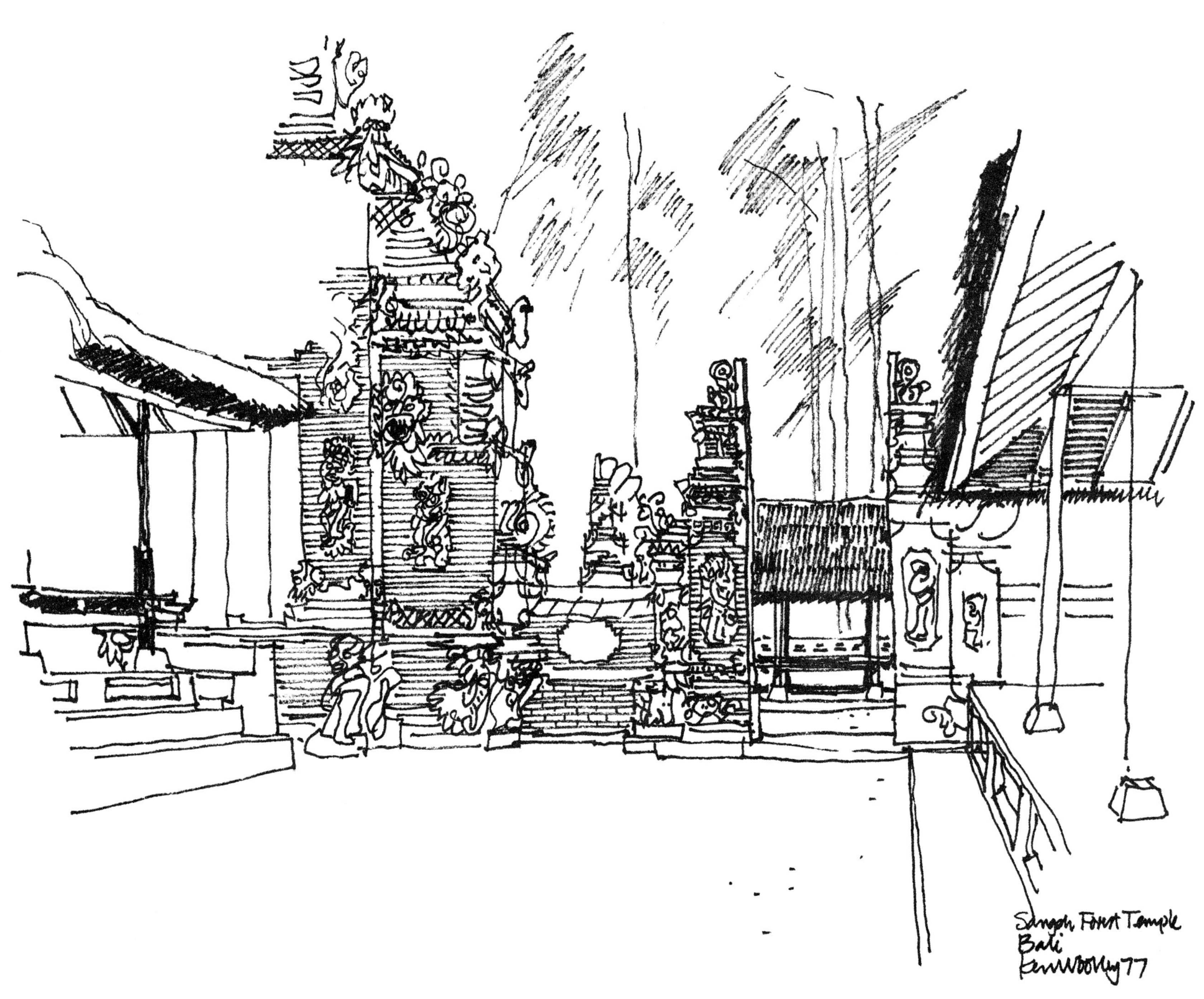

17

Sangeh Forest Temple, Bali 1977

Pentel, Ingres paper 23.5 x 29.5

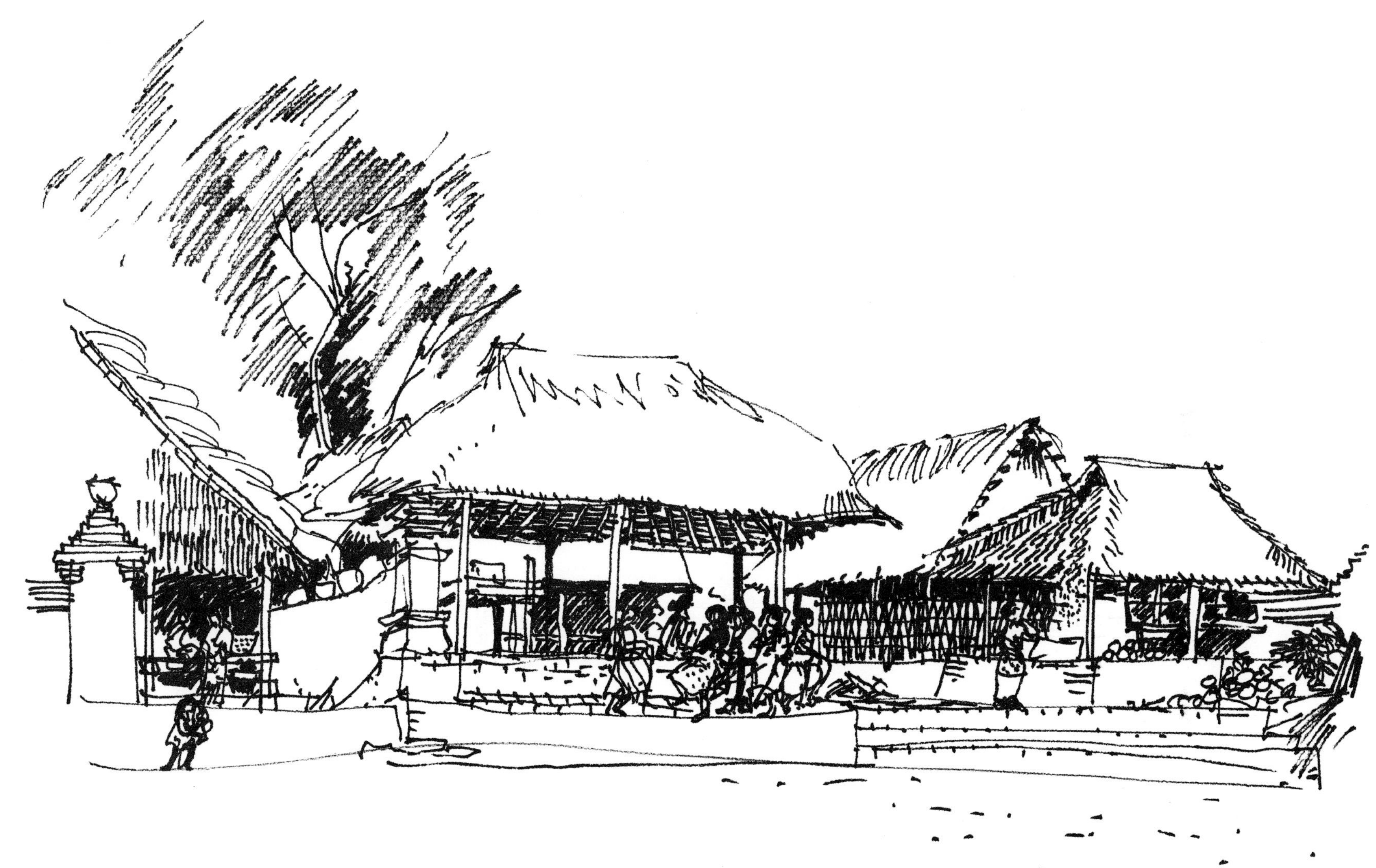

18

Tampaksiring, Bali 1977

Pentel, Ingres paper 23.5 x 29.5 Exhibited

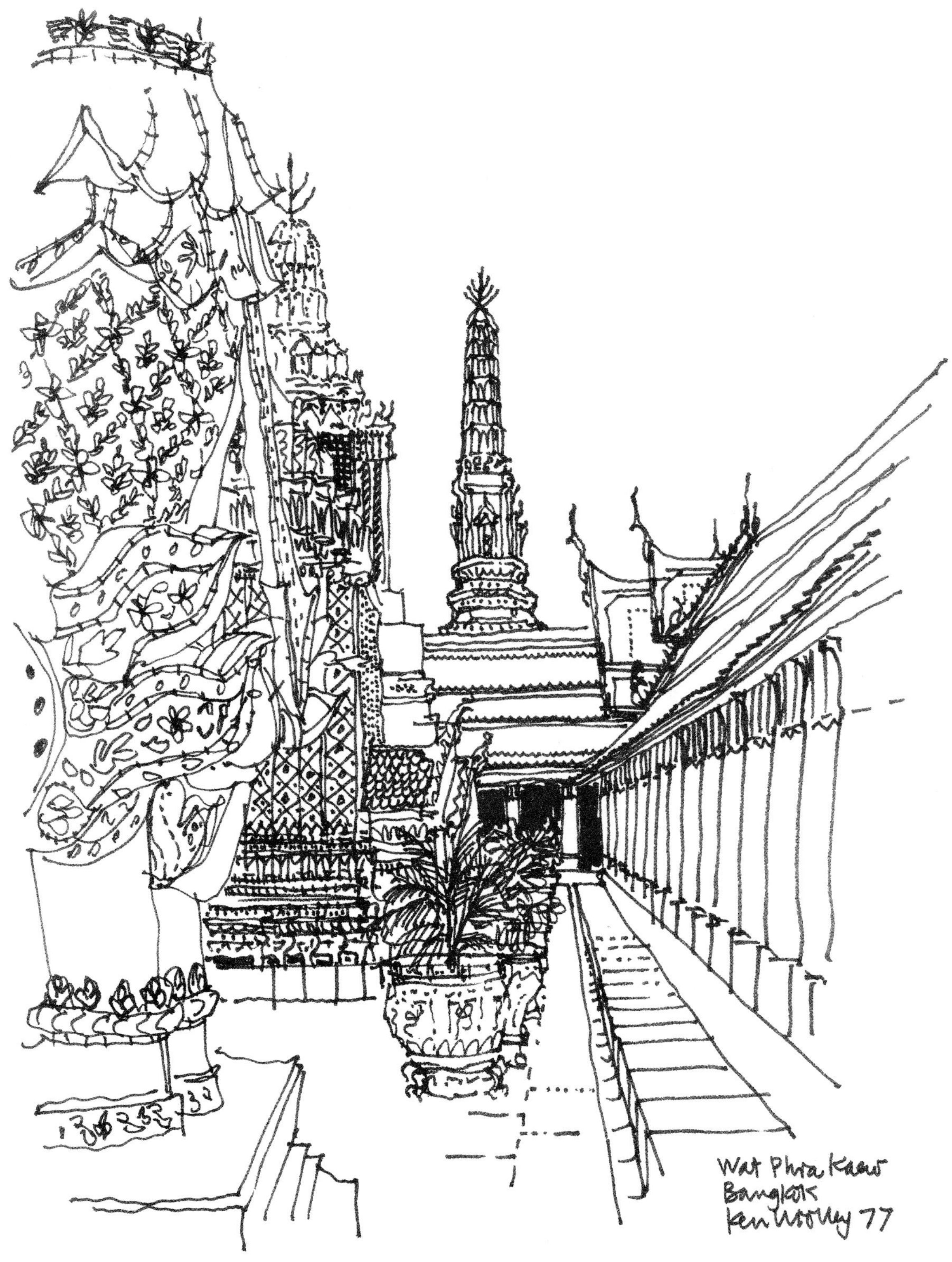

The Emerald Buddha Temple, Giant Guardians, Wat Phra Kaew, Bangkok 1977

Pentel, cartridge paper 17.5 x 24.5 Exhibited

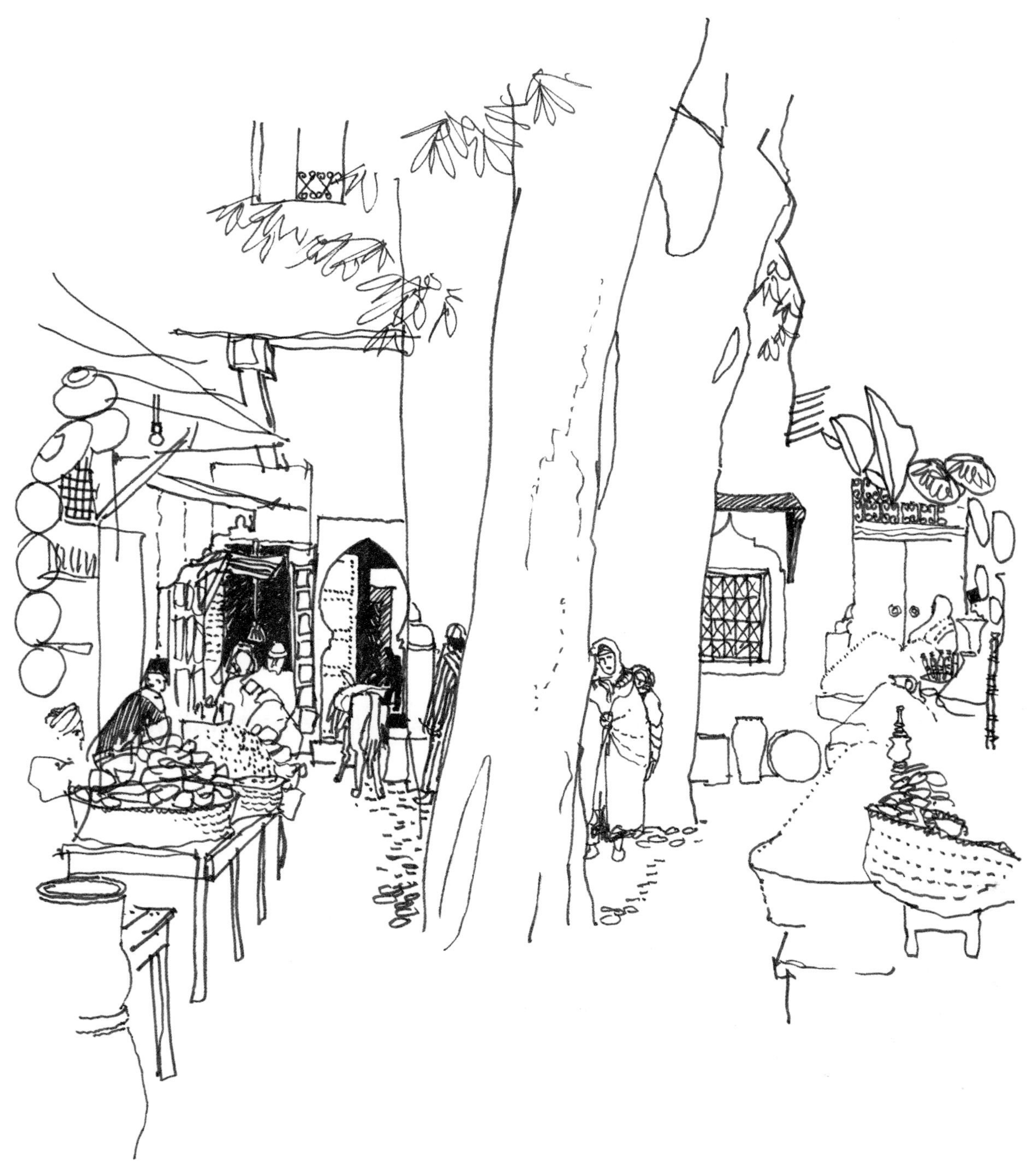

Henna Souk. Fez
Ken Woolley 77

20

Henna Souk, Fez, Morocco 1977

Pentel, cartridge paper 27.5 x 35.5

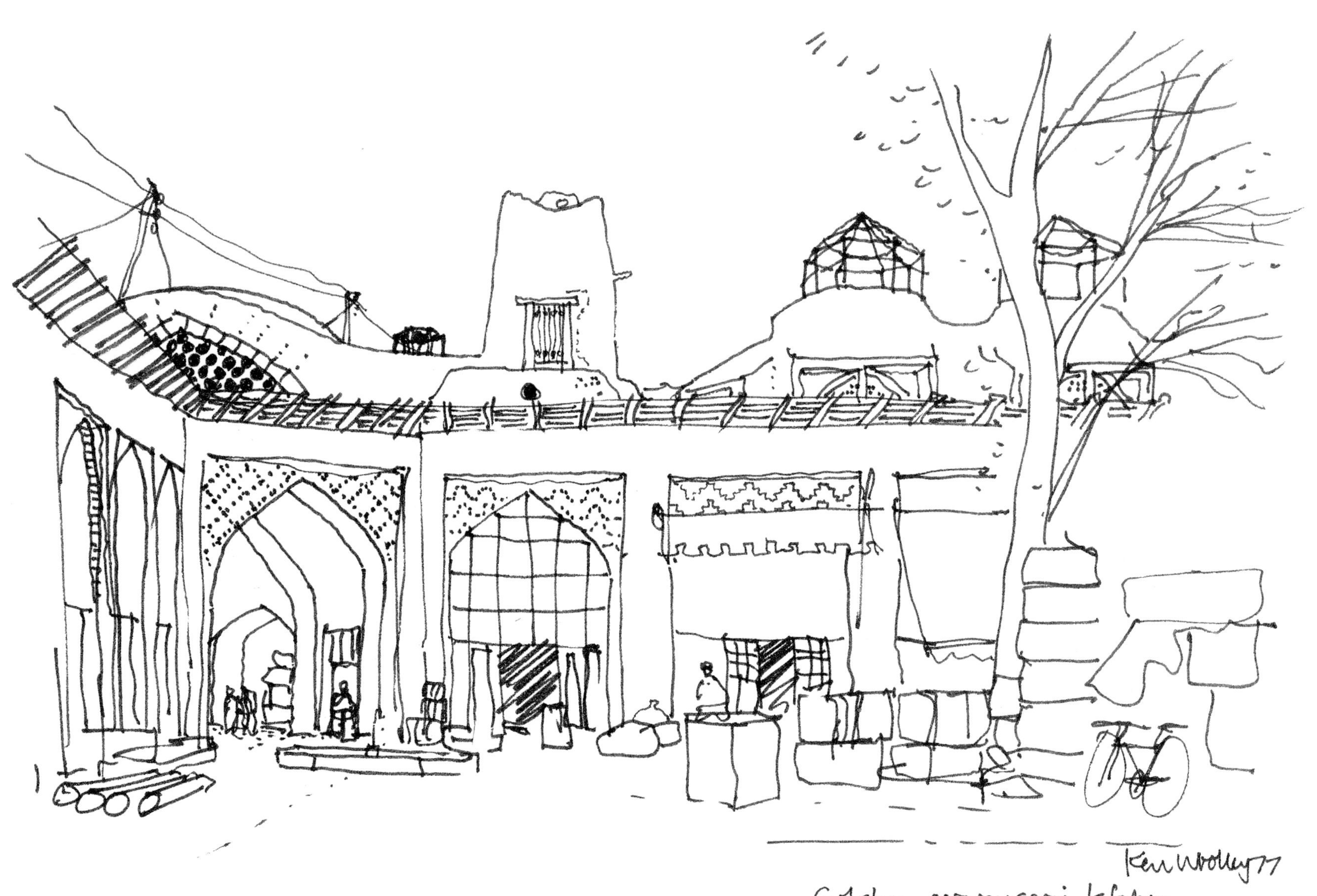

21
Caravanserai, Isfahan, Iran 1977
Pentel, cartridge paper 17.5 x 24.5 Exhibited

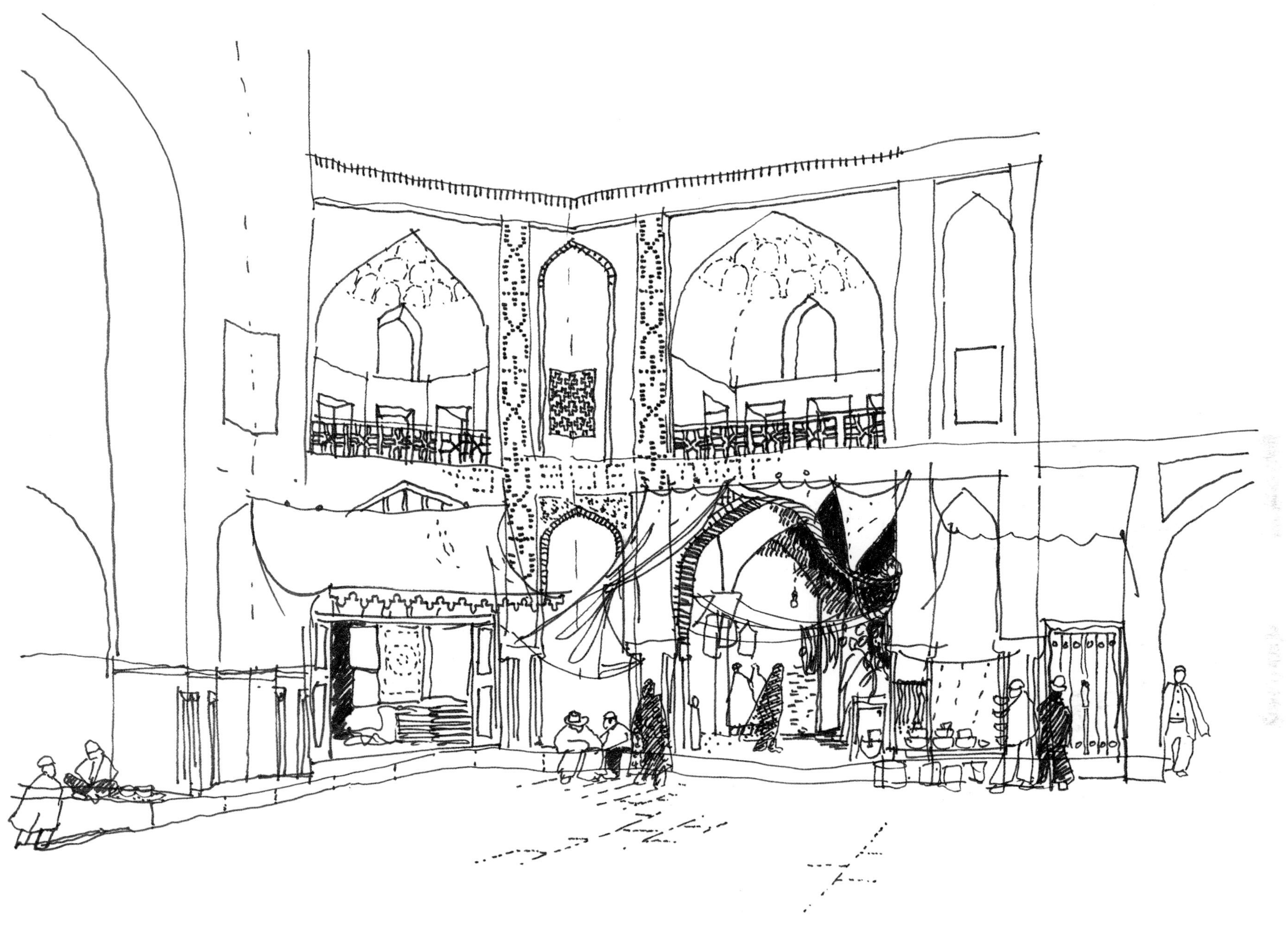

Qaysariya Gate, Side Bazaar, Isfahan, Iran 1977

Pentel, cartridge paper 27.5 x 35.5

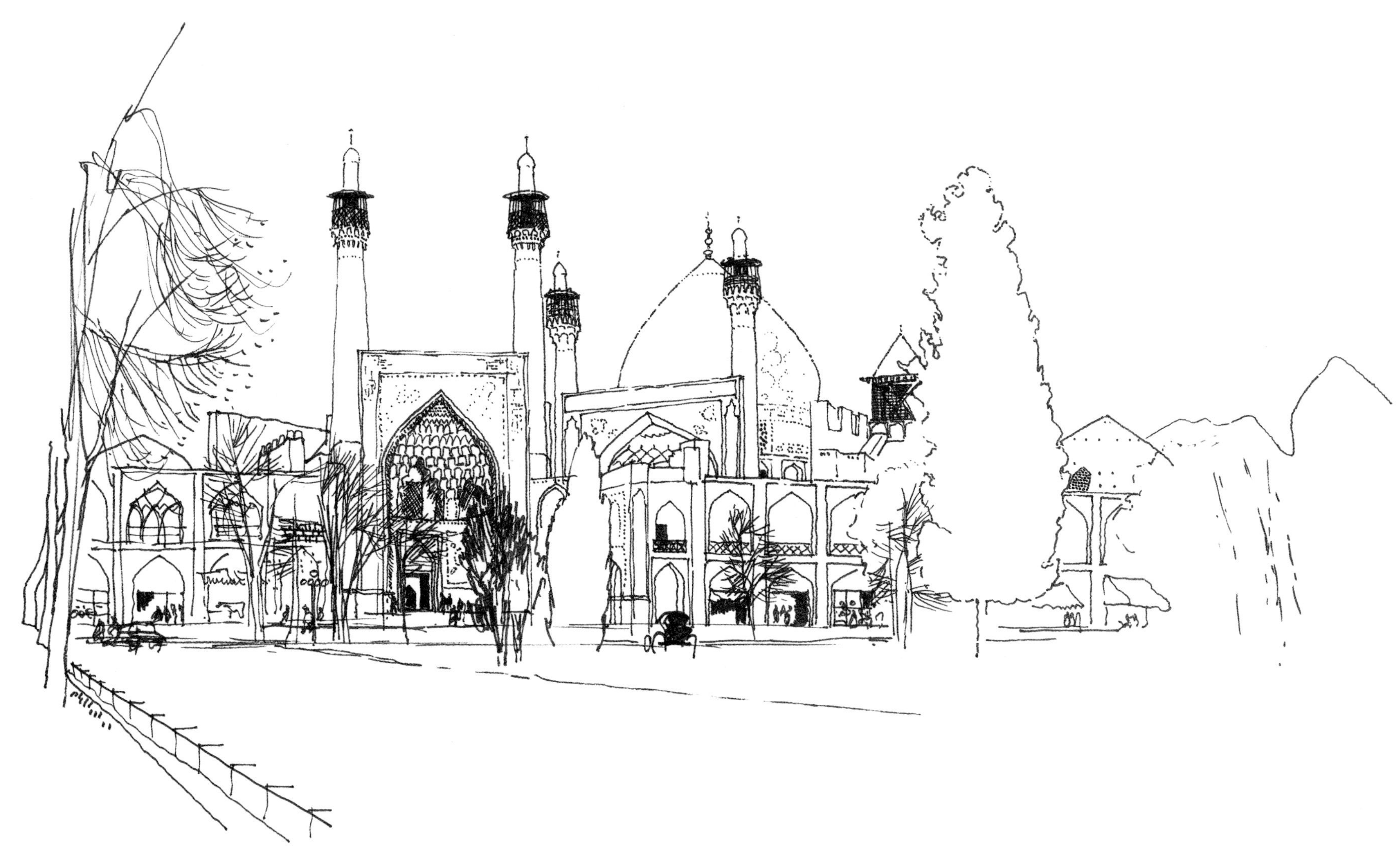

23

Great Mosque and Medan, Isfahan, Iran 1977

Pentel, cartridge paper 27.5 x 35.5

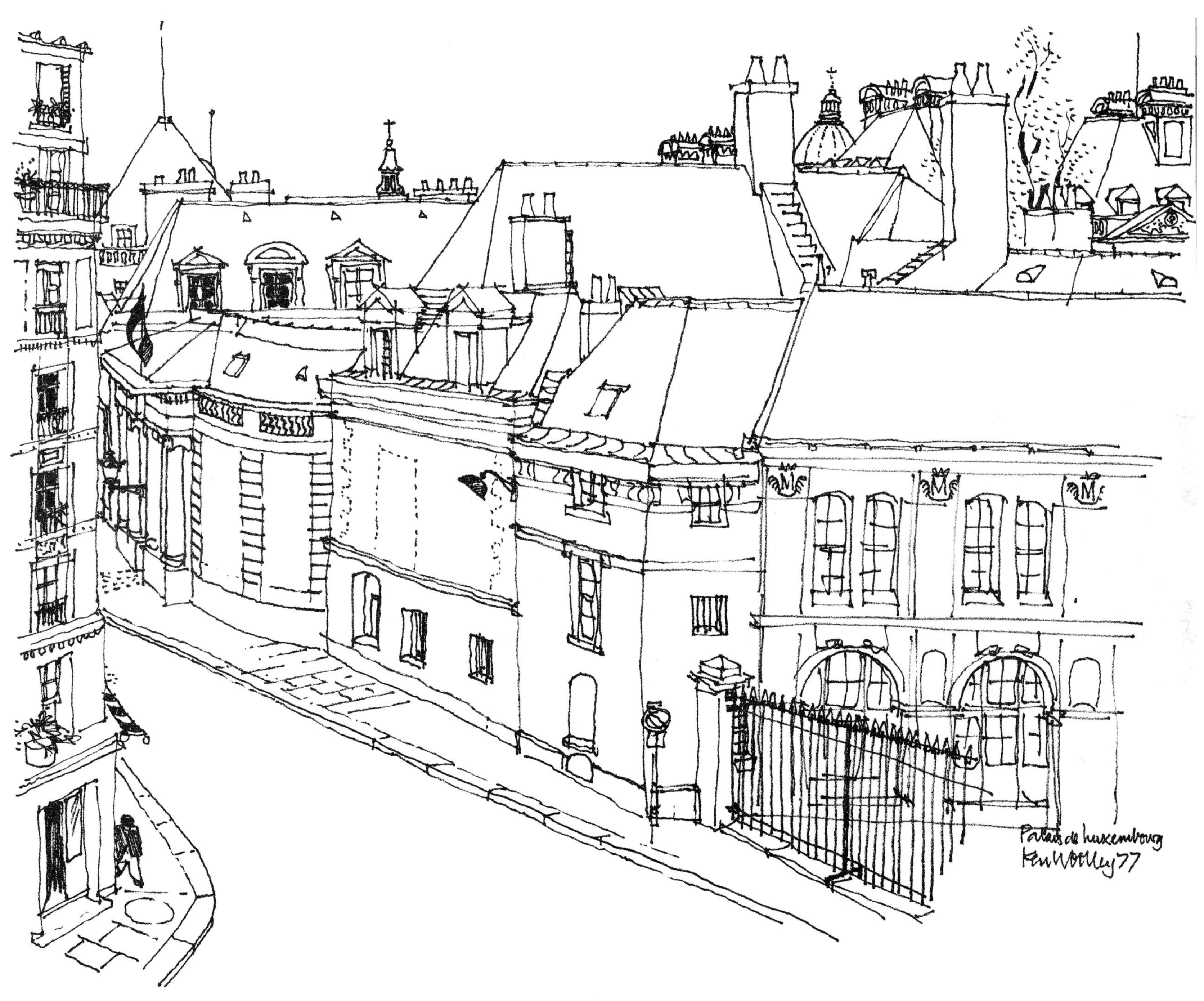

24

Palais de Luxembourg, Paris 1977

Pentel, Ingres paper 23.5 x 29.5 Exhibited

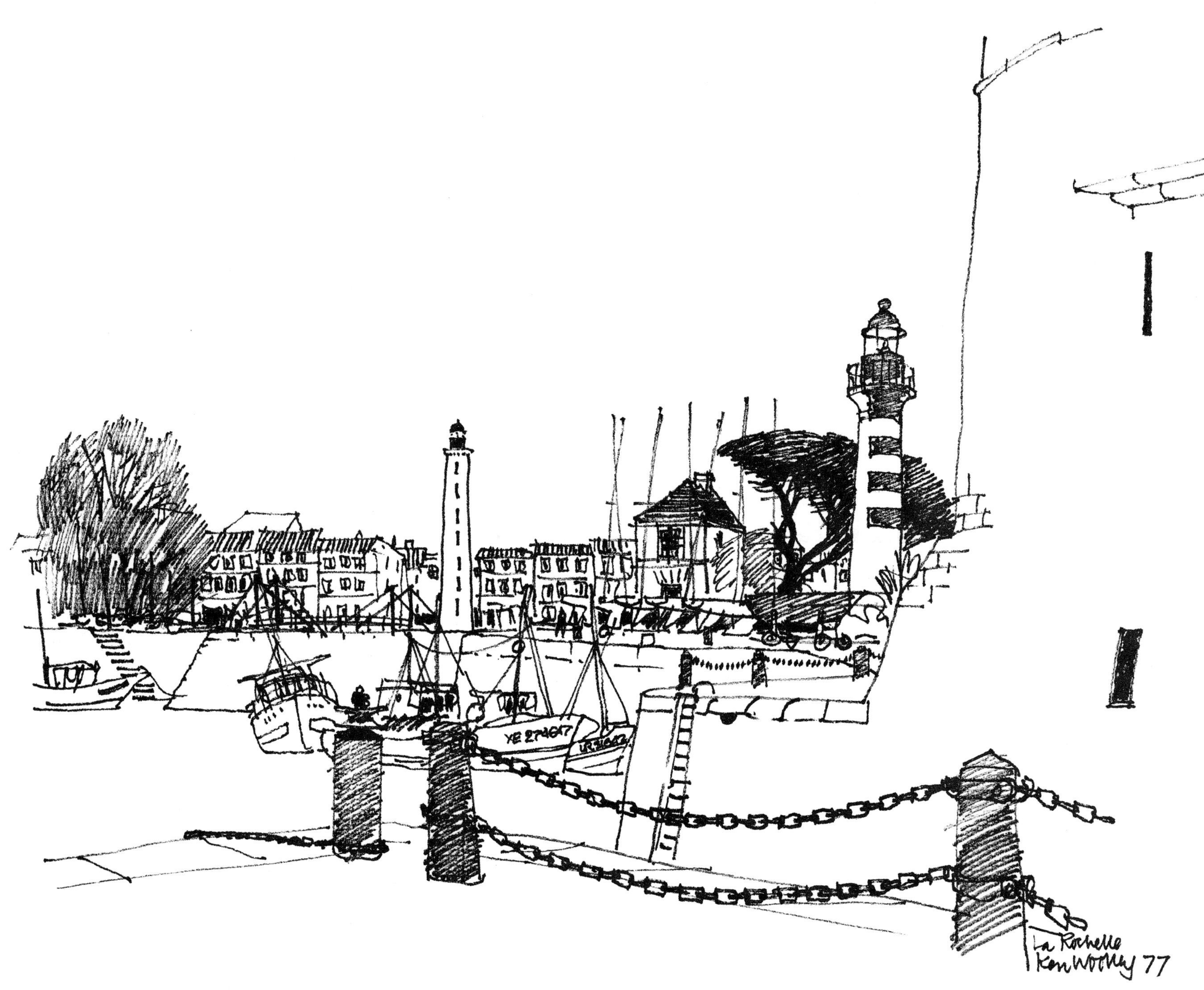

25

La Rochelle, France 1977

Pentel, Ingres paper 23.5 x 29.5 Exhibited

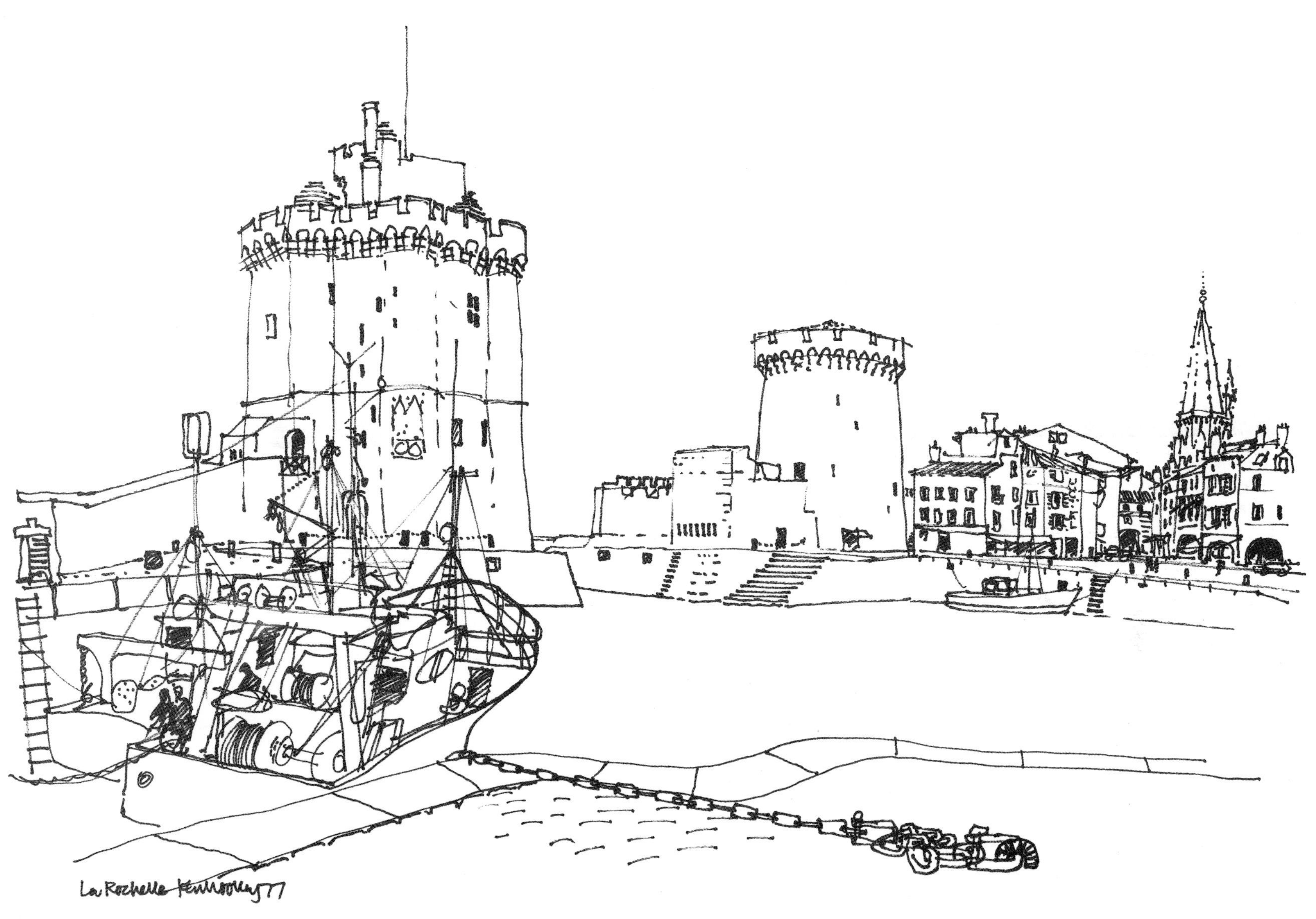

26

La Rochelle, France 1977

Pentel, cartridge paper 27 x 36.5

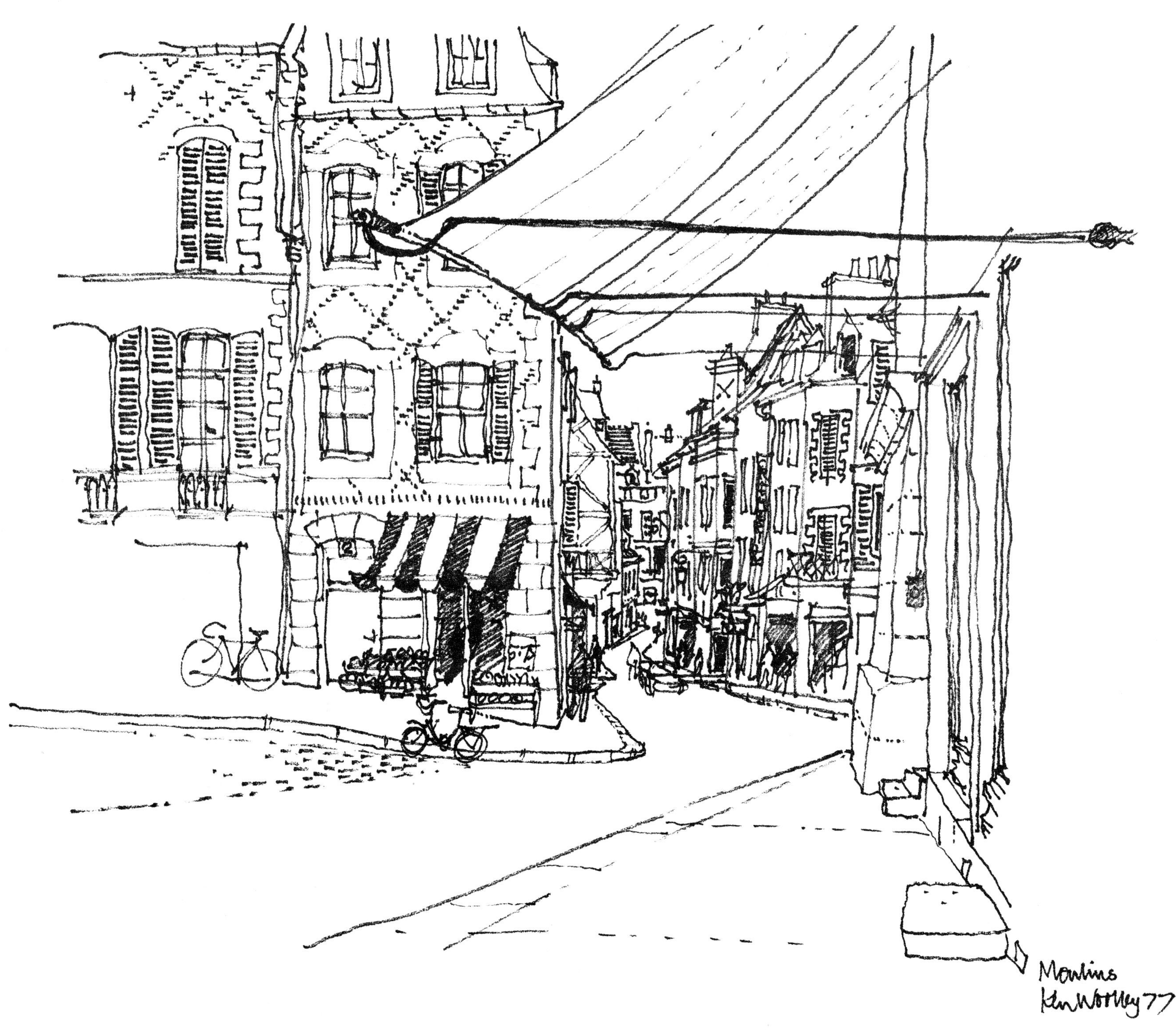

27
Moulins, France 1977
Pentel, Ingres paper 23.5 x 29.5 Exhibited

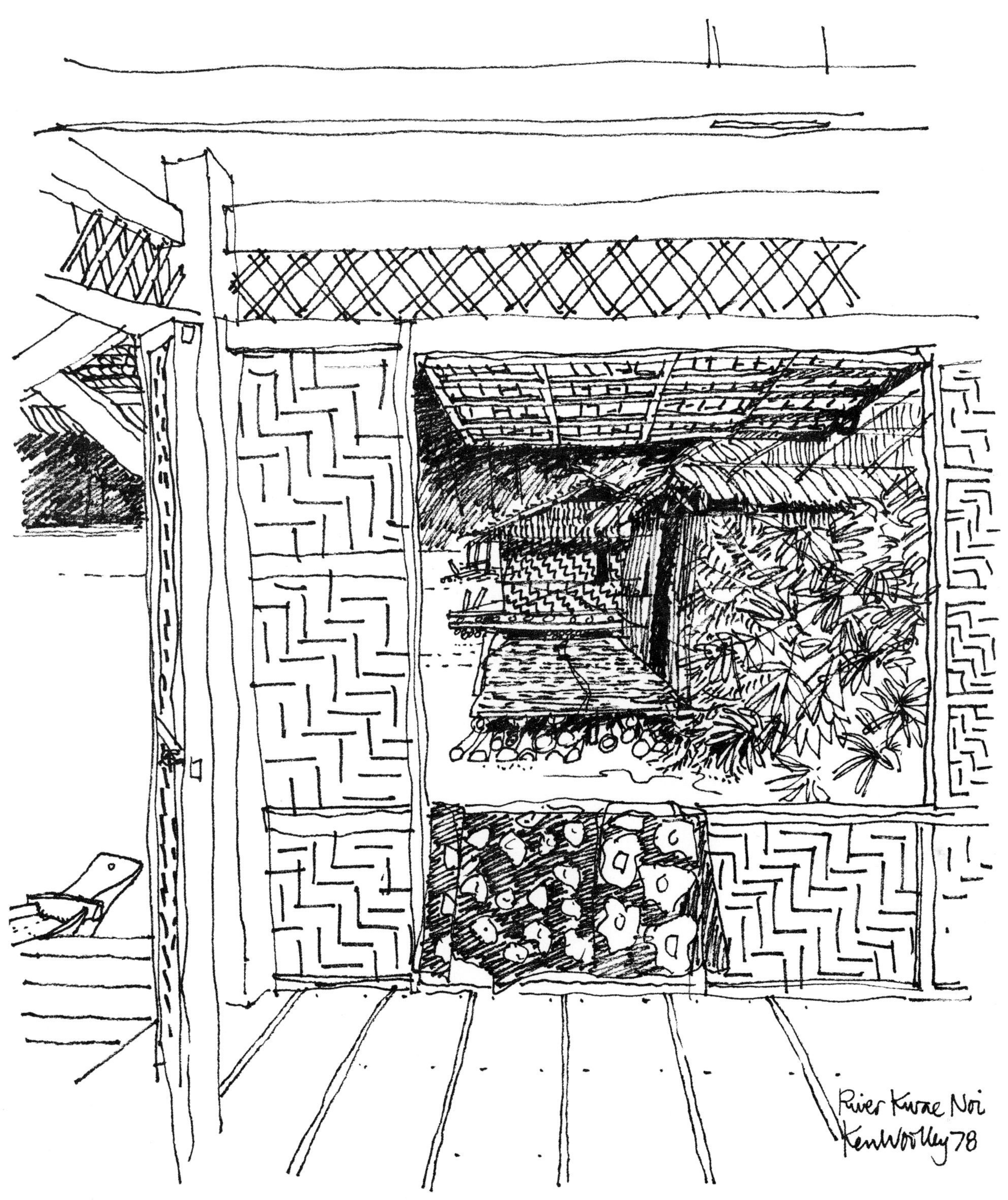

River Kwai Noi, Thailand 1978

Pentel, Ingres paper 23.5 x 29.5

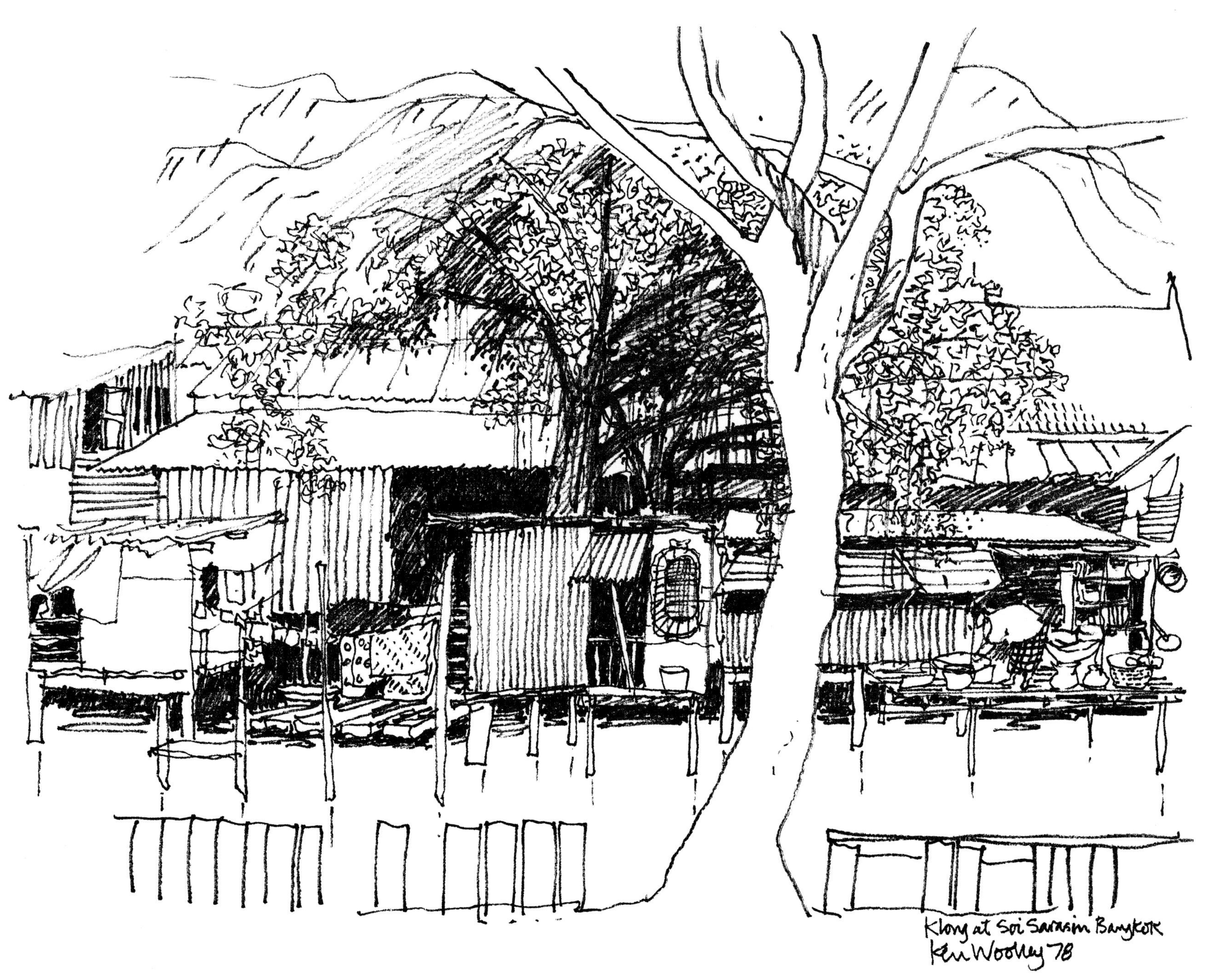

Klong at Soi Sarasin, Bangkok 1978

Pentel, Ingres paper 23.5 x 29.5

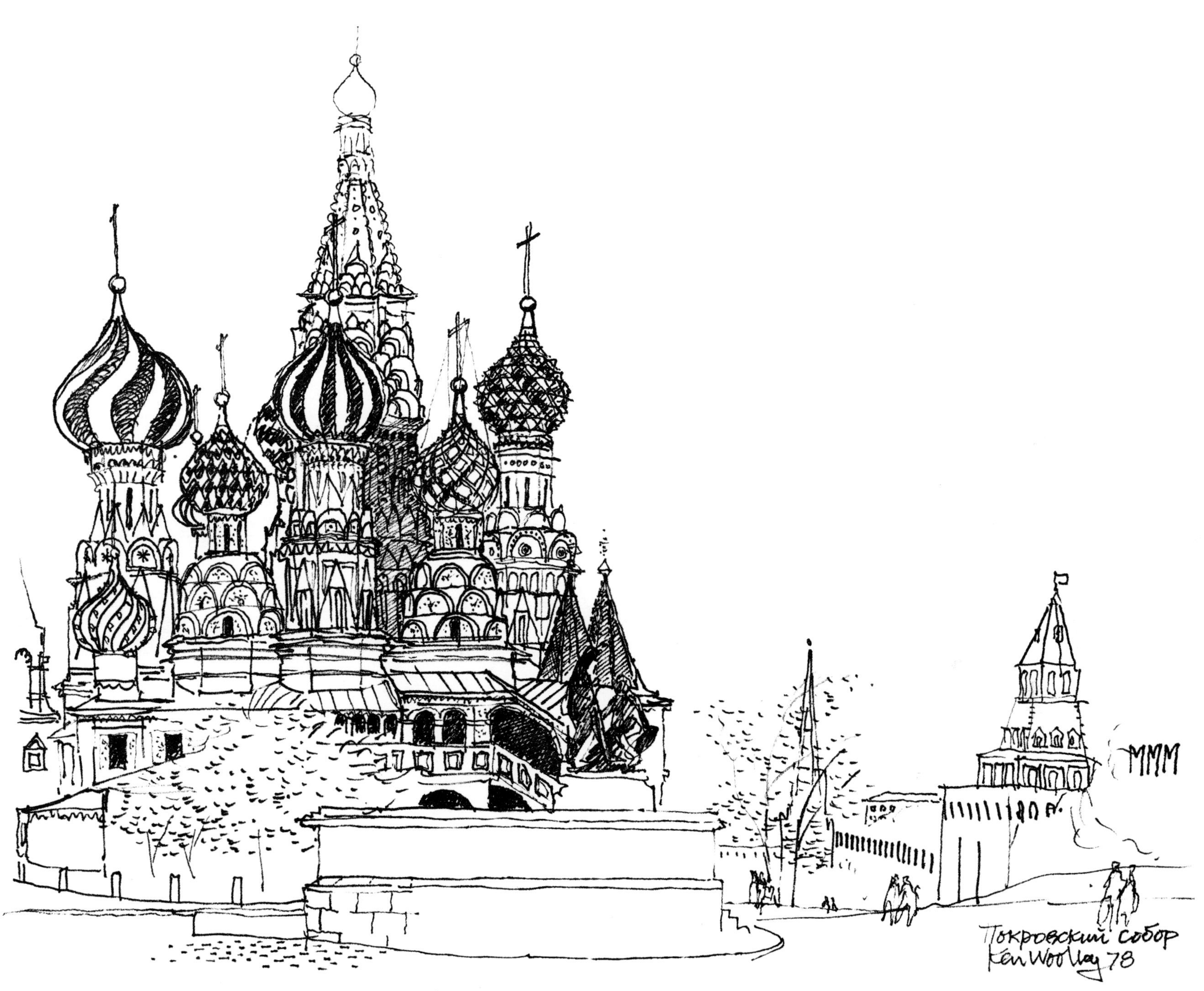

Pokrovsky Sobor (St. Basils), Moscow 1978

Pentel, Ingres paper 23.5 x 29.5 Exhibited

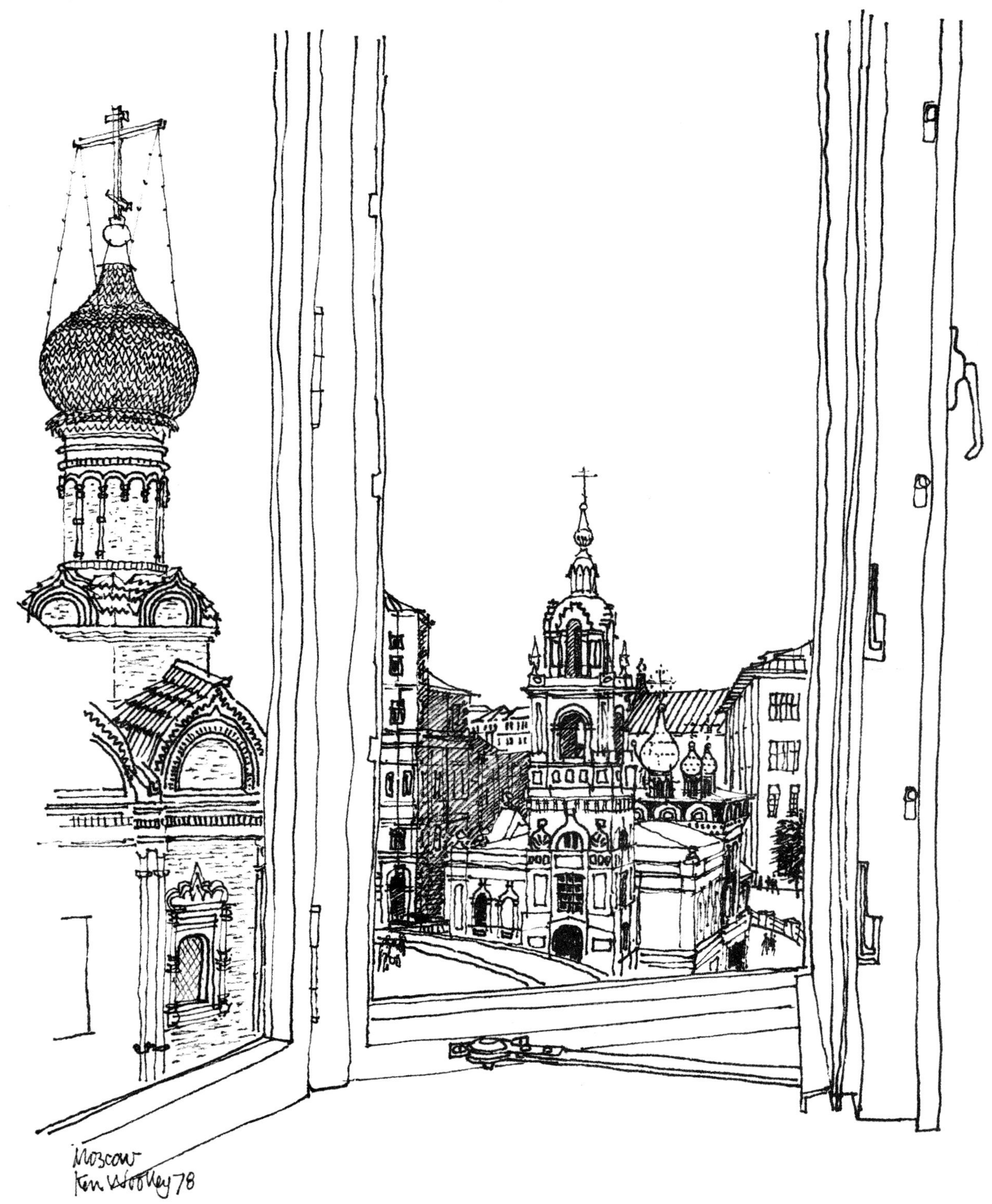

31

Moscow from the Rossia Hotel, 1978

Pentel, Ingres paper 23.5 x 29 Exhibited

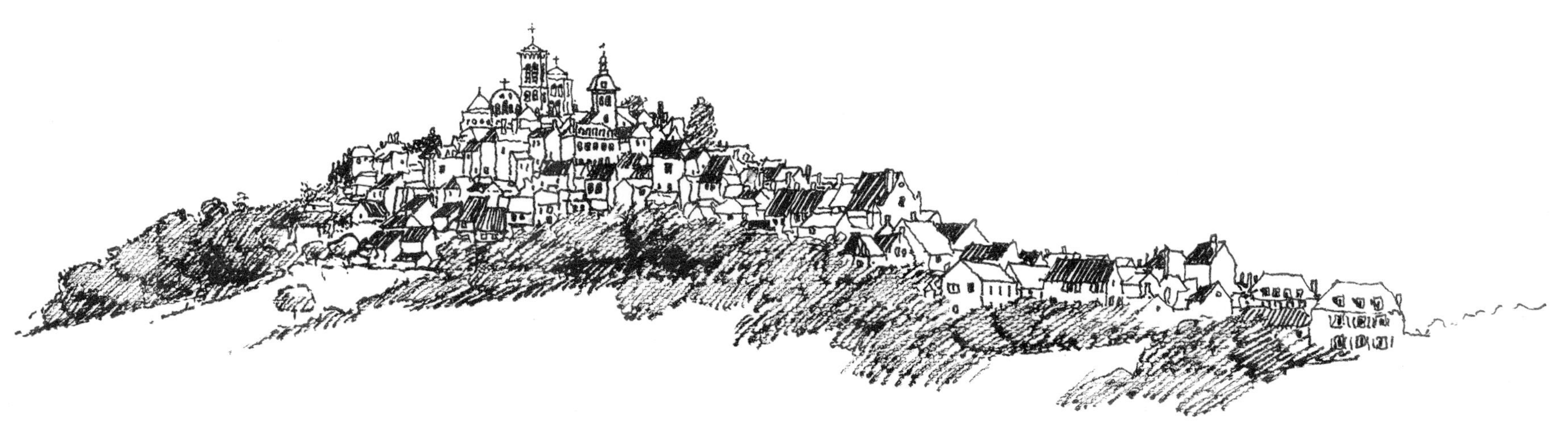

32

Vezelay, Burgundy, France 1978

Pentel, heavy water colour paper 21 x 29 Exhibited

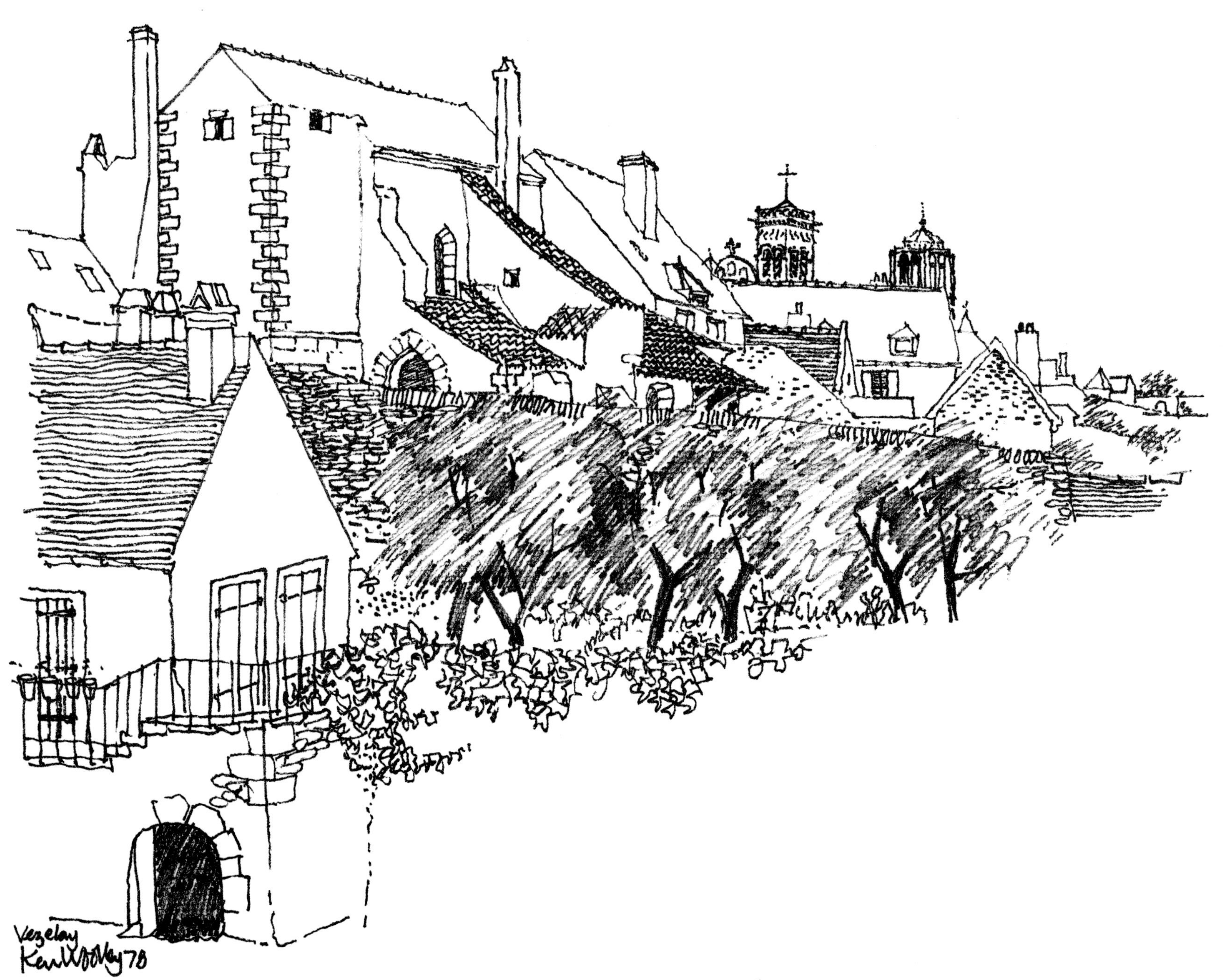

33

Vezelay, Burgundy, France 1978

Pentel, Ingres paper 23.5 x 29.5

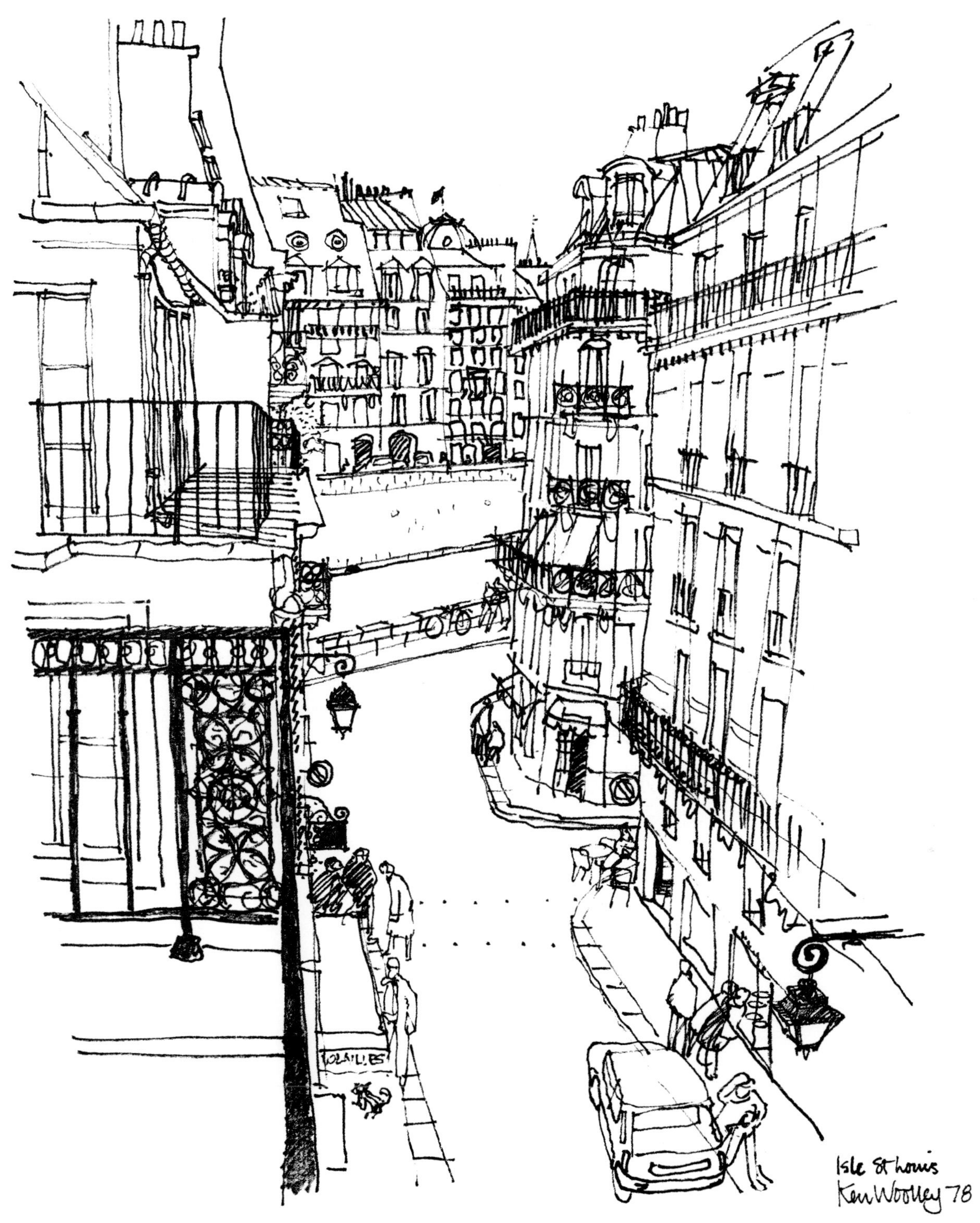

34

Isle S. Louis, Paris 1978

Pentel, Ingres paper 23.5 x 29.5 Exhibited

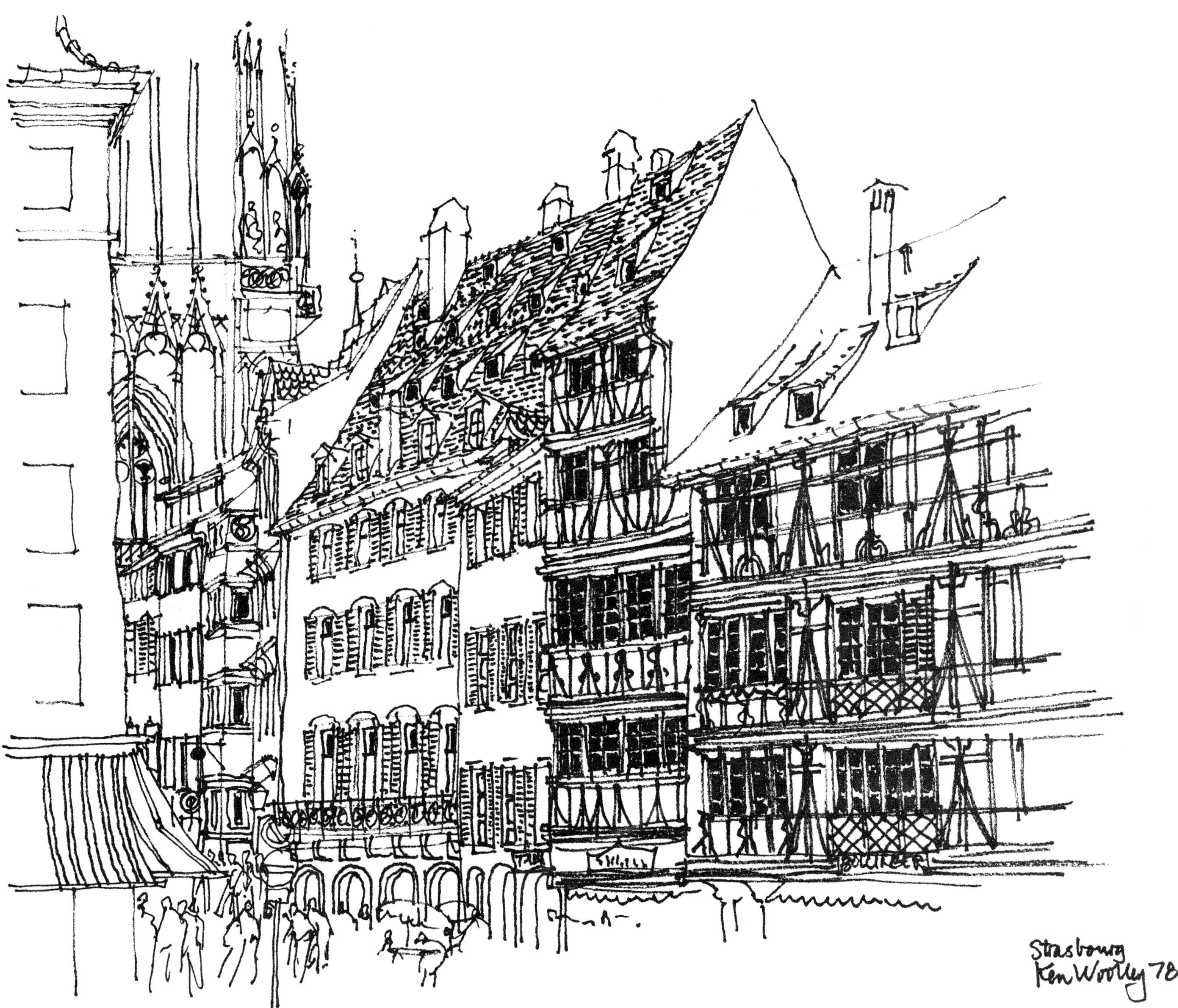

35

Strasbourg Cathedral, France 1978

Pentel, Ingres paper 23.5 x 29.5 Exhibited

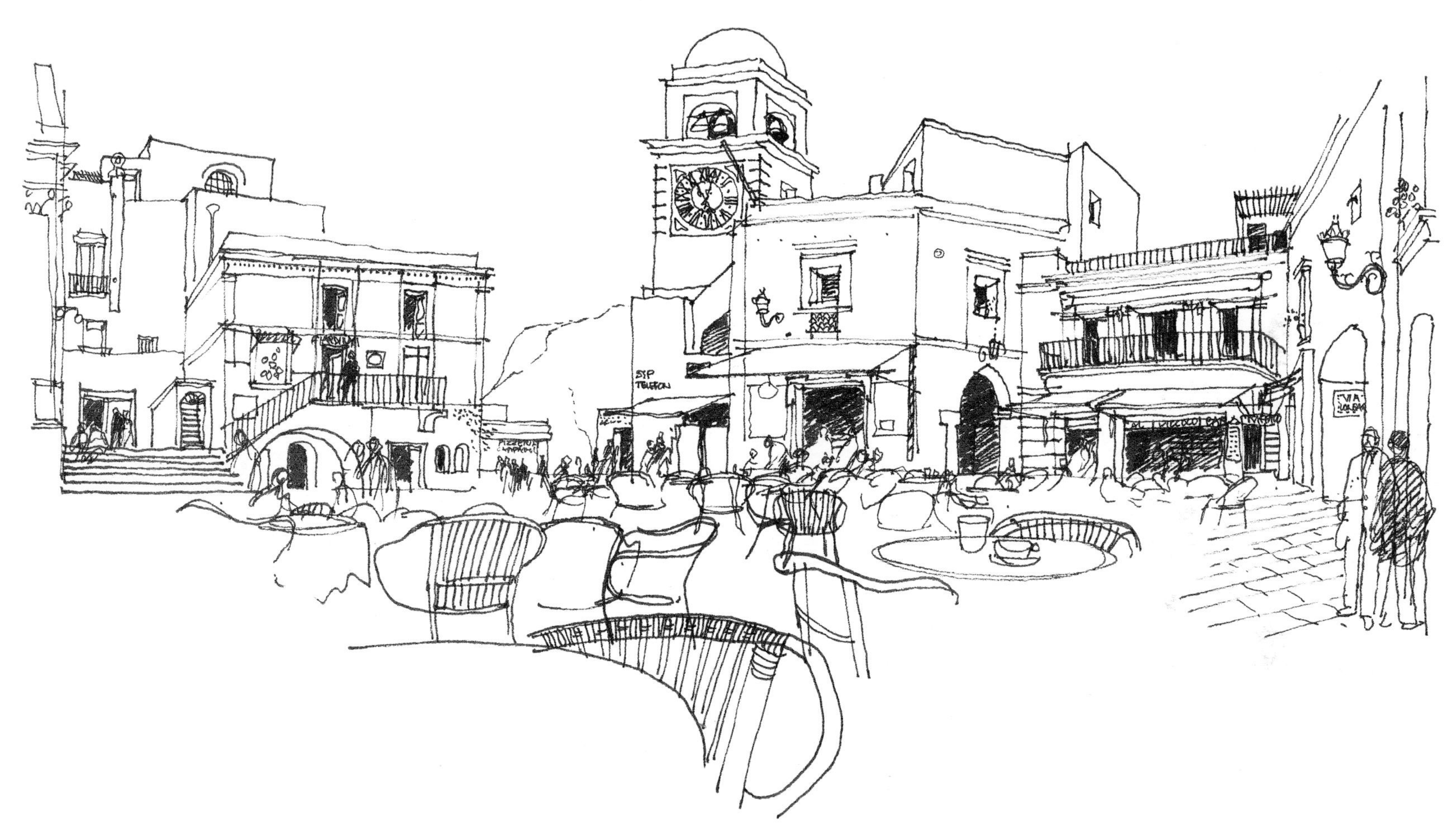

Capri
Ken Woolley 79

36
Piazza Umberto 1, Capri, Italy 1979
Pentel, cartridge paper 27 x 36.5 Exhibited

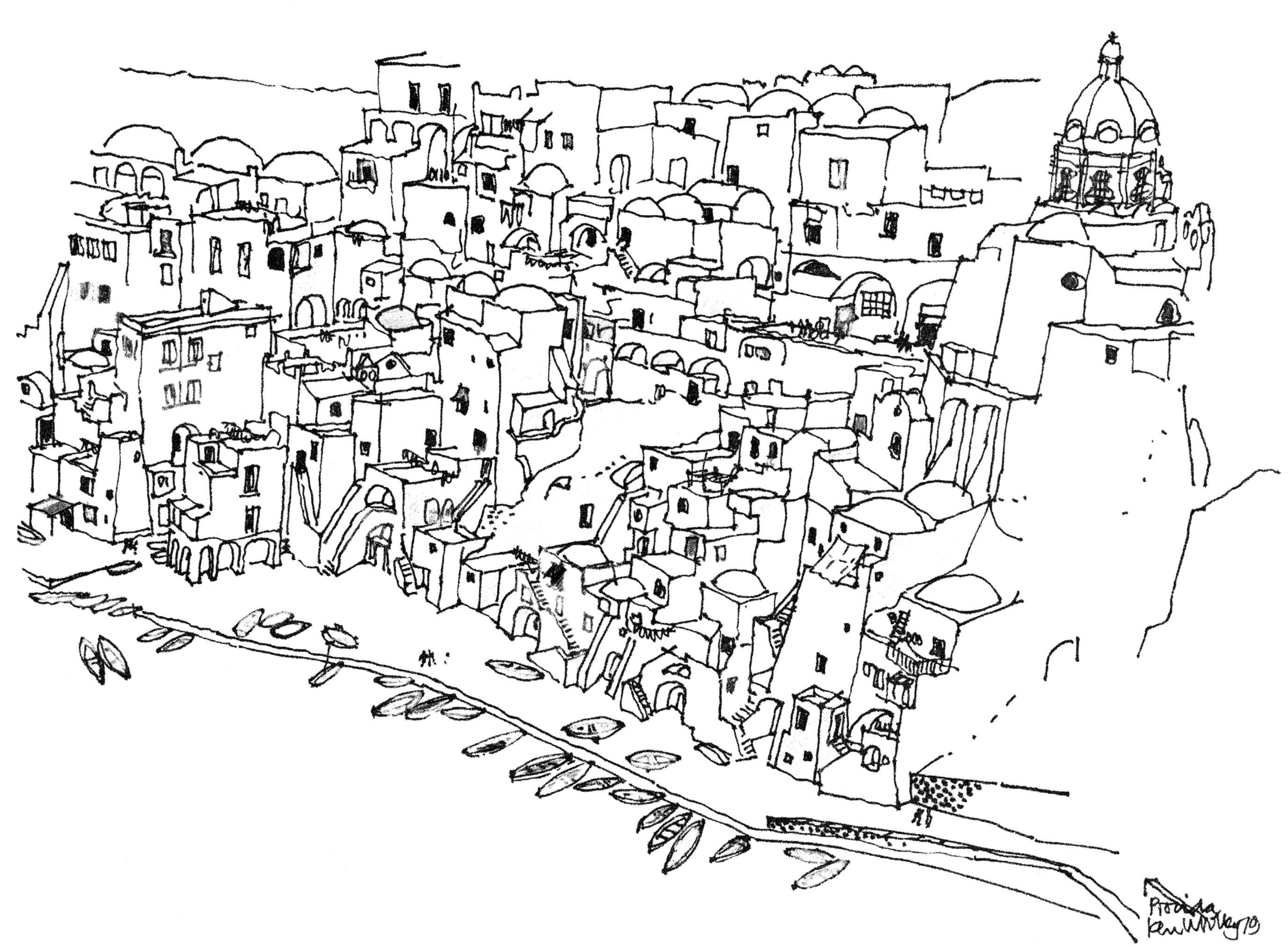

37

The Island of Procida, Italy 1979

Pentel, cartridge paper 17.5 x 24.5

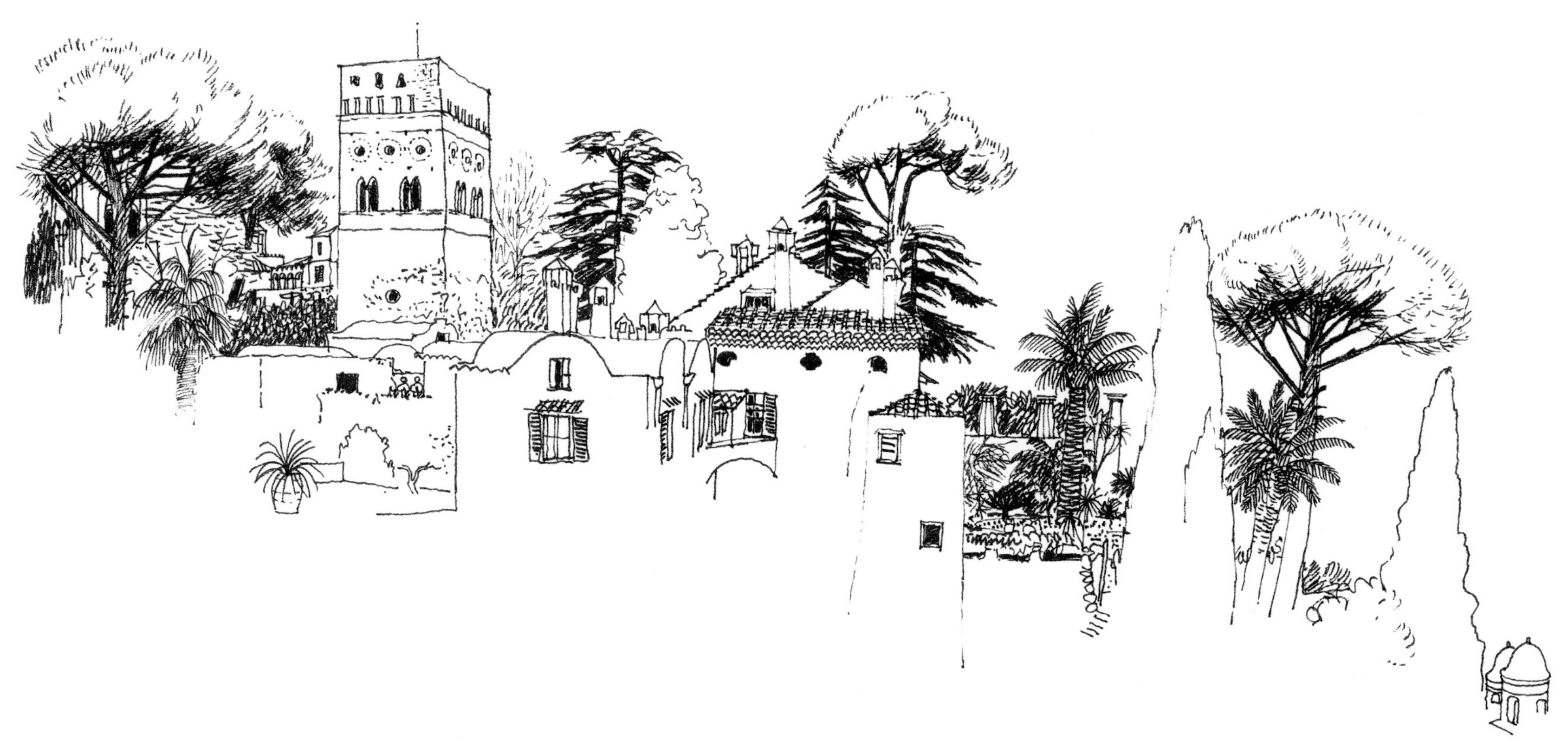

Villa Rufolo, Ravello
Ken Woolley 79

38

Villa Rufolo, Ravello, Italy 1979

Pentel, cartridge paper 27 x 36.5 Exhibited

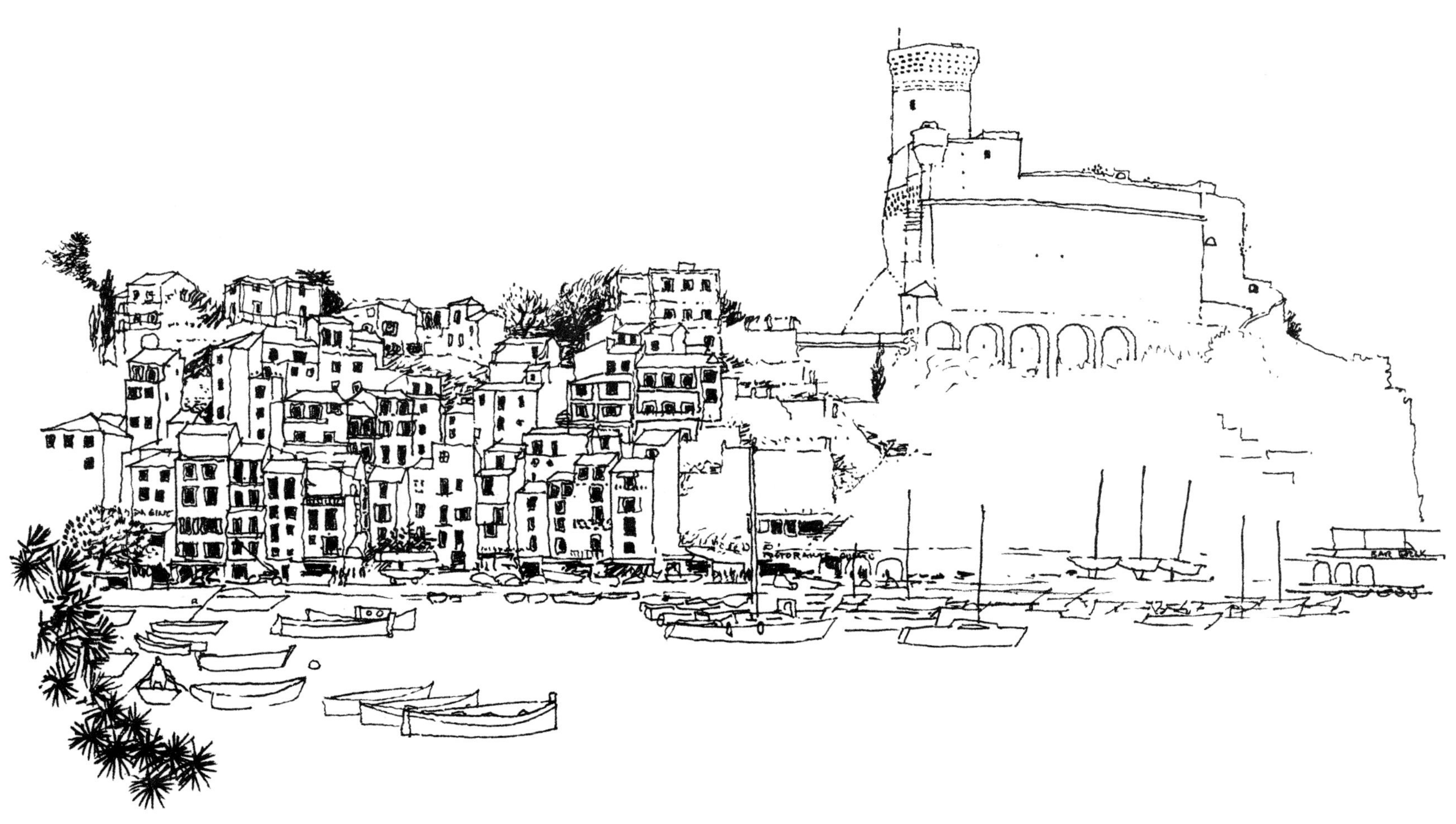

Lerici
Ken Woolley 81

39

Lerici, Italy 1981

Pentel, cartridge paper 24.5 x 27 Exhibited

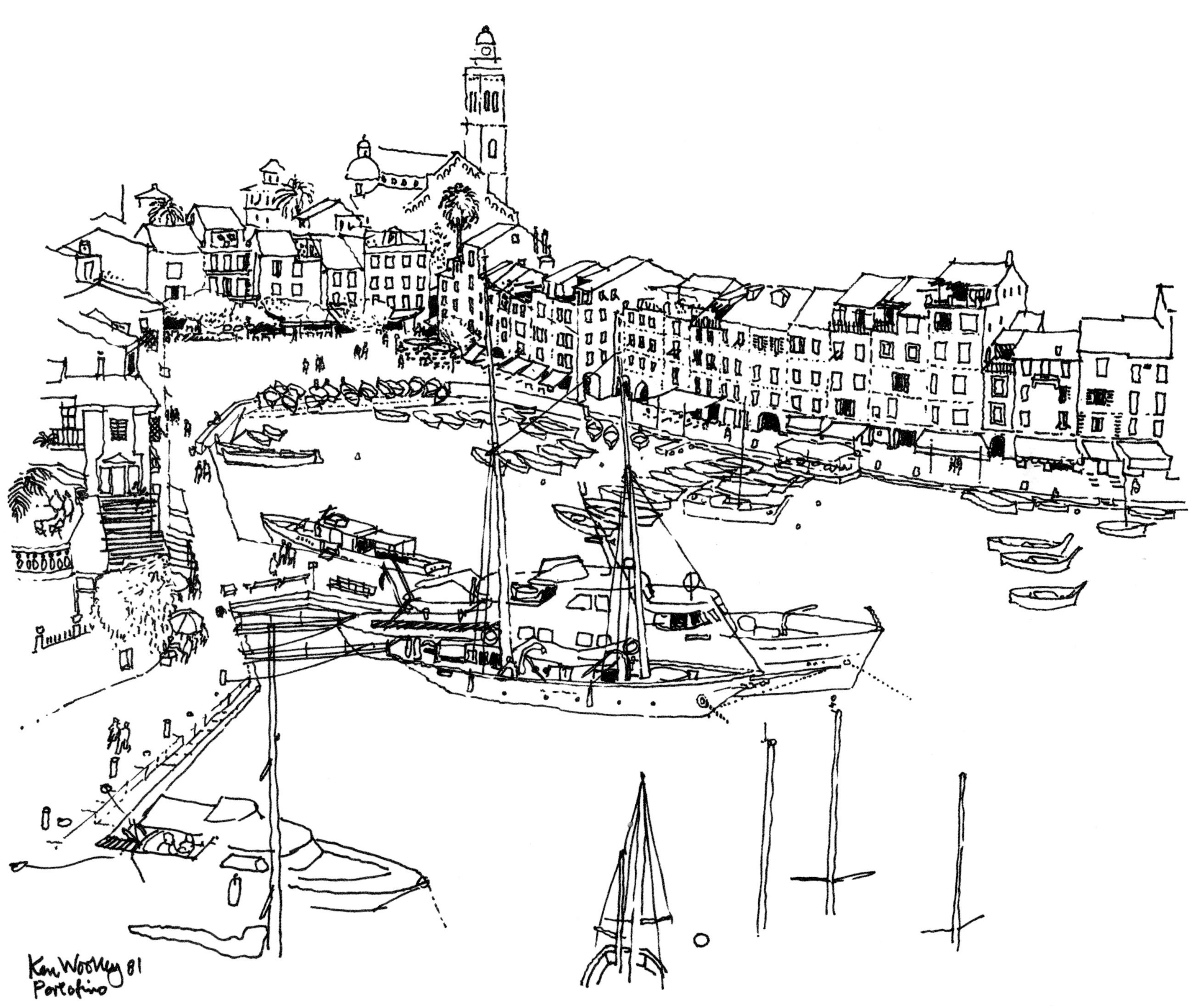

Portofino, Italy 1981

Pentel, cartridge paper 23 x 27

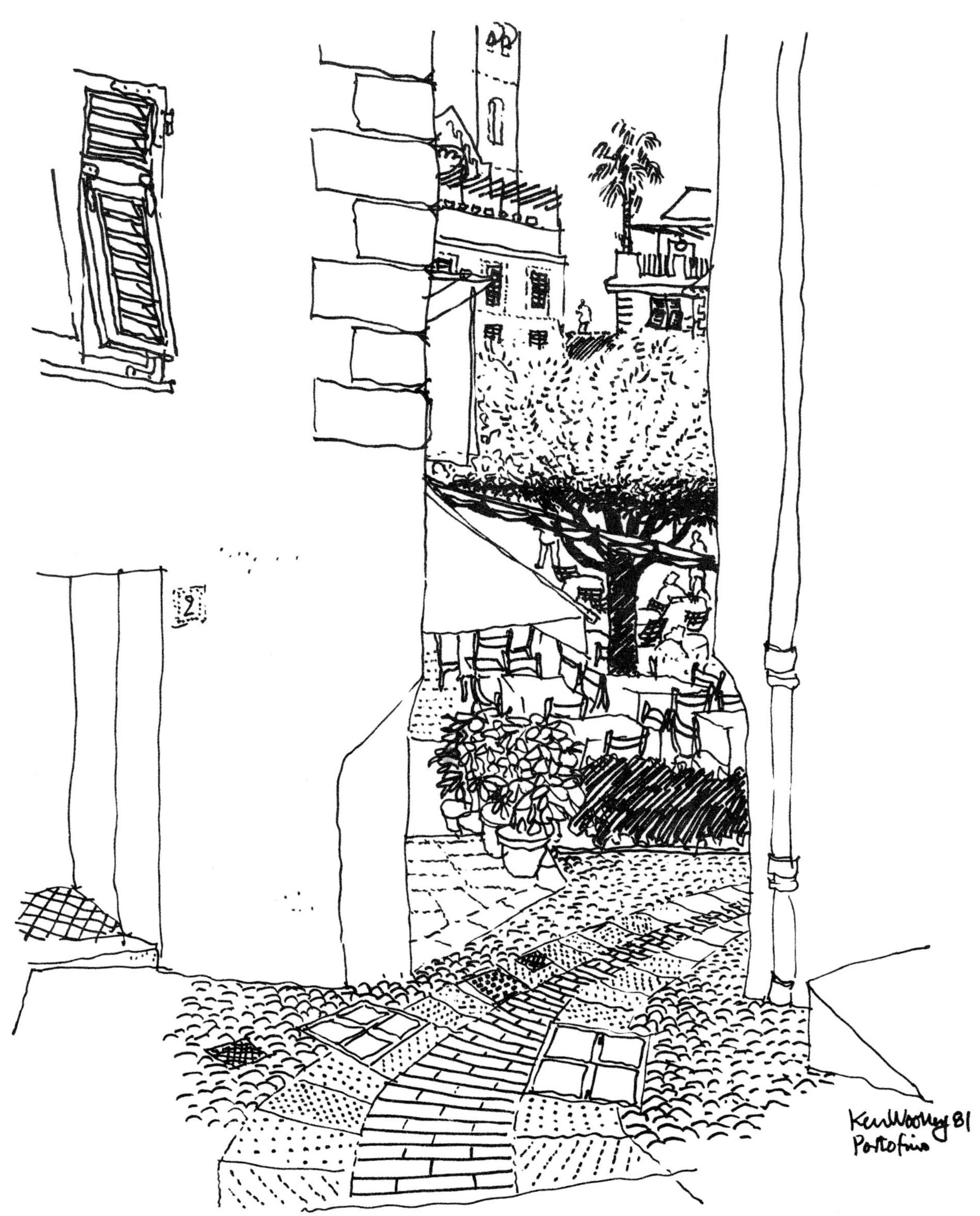

41

Sidestreet, Portofino, Italy 1981

Pentel, cartridge paper 23 x 27

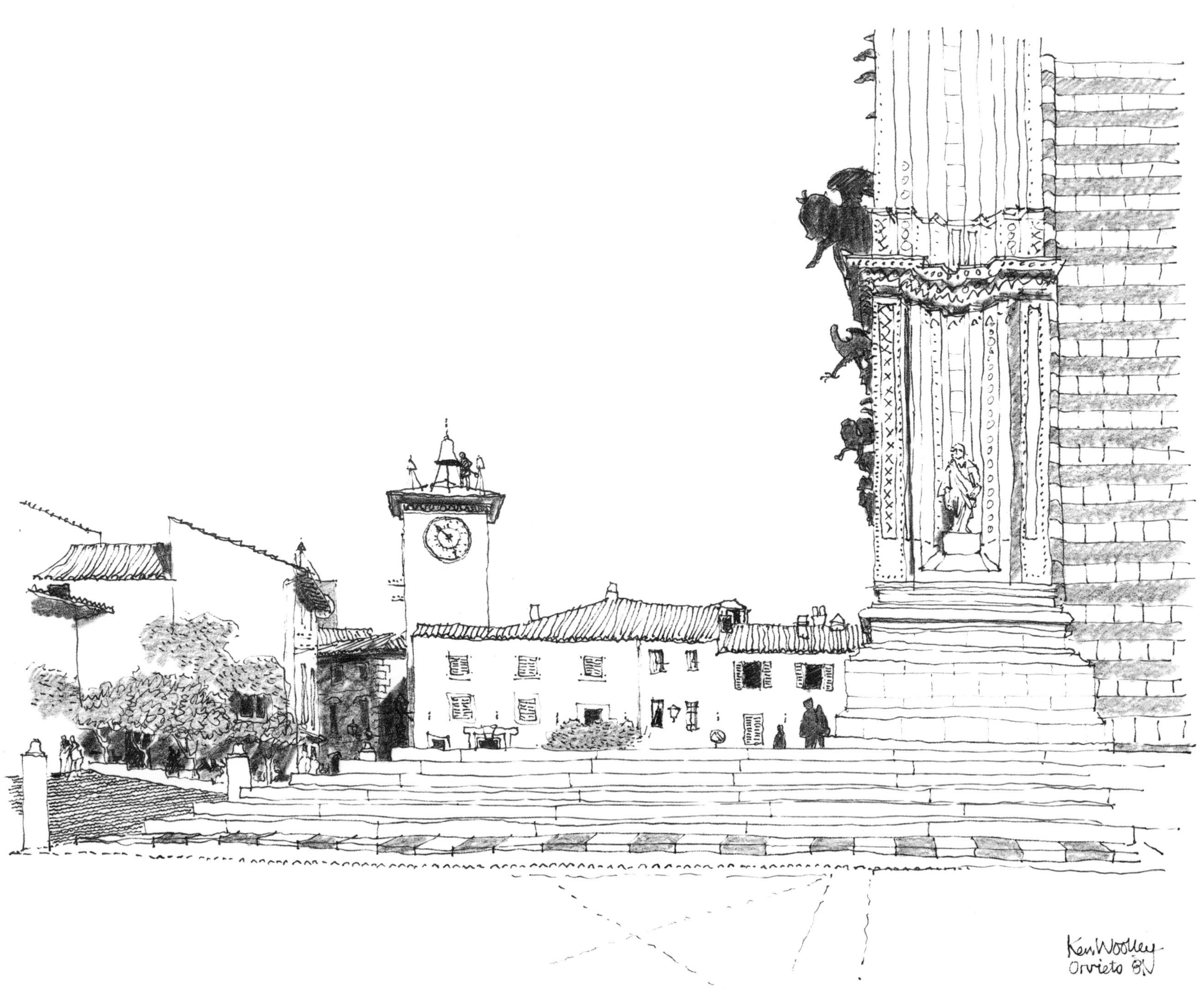

Orvieto, Italy 1981

Fountain pen, Indian ink, carbon pencil, cartridge paper 23 x 27

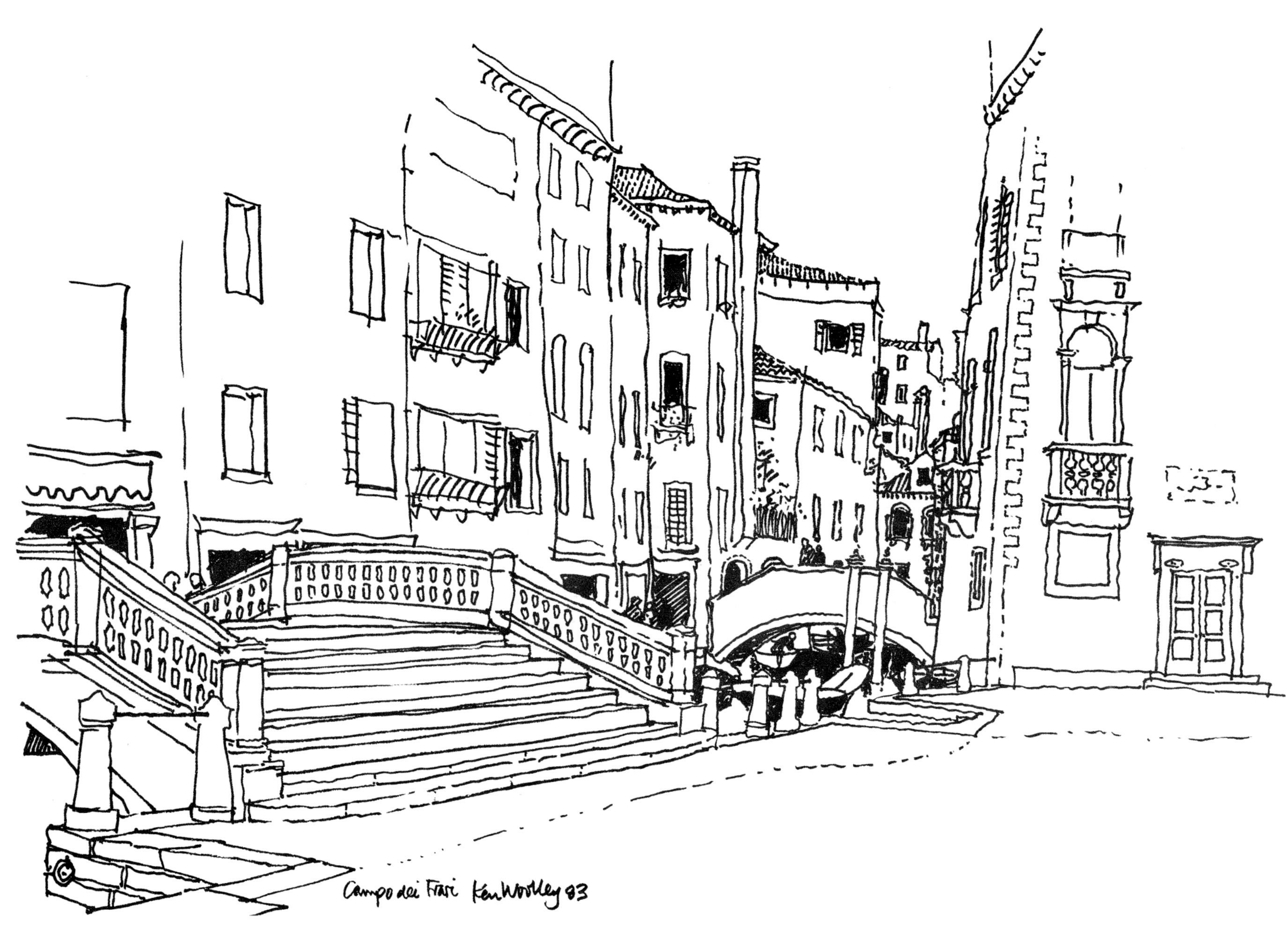

Campo dei Fiori, Venice 1983

Pentel, cartridge paper 21 x 29.5

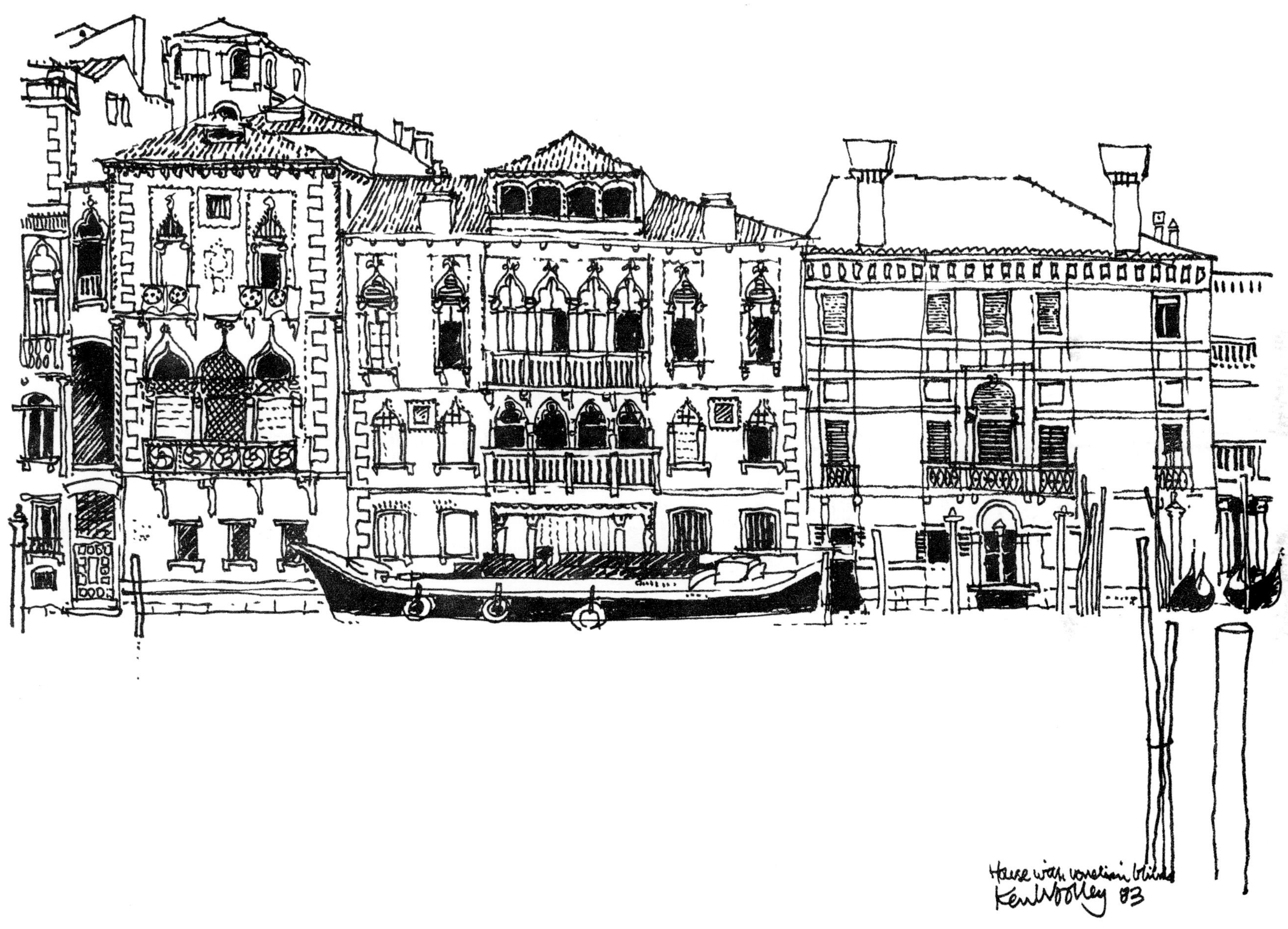

44

House with venetian blinds, Venice 1983

Pentel, cartridge paper 23 x 27

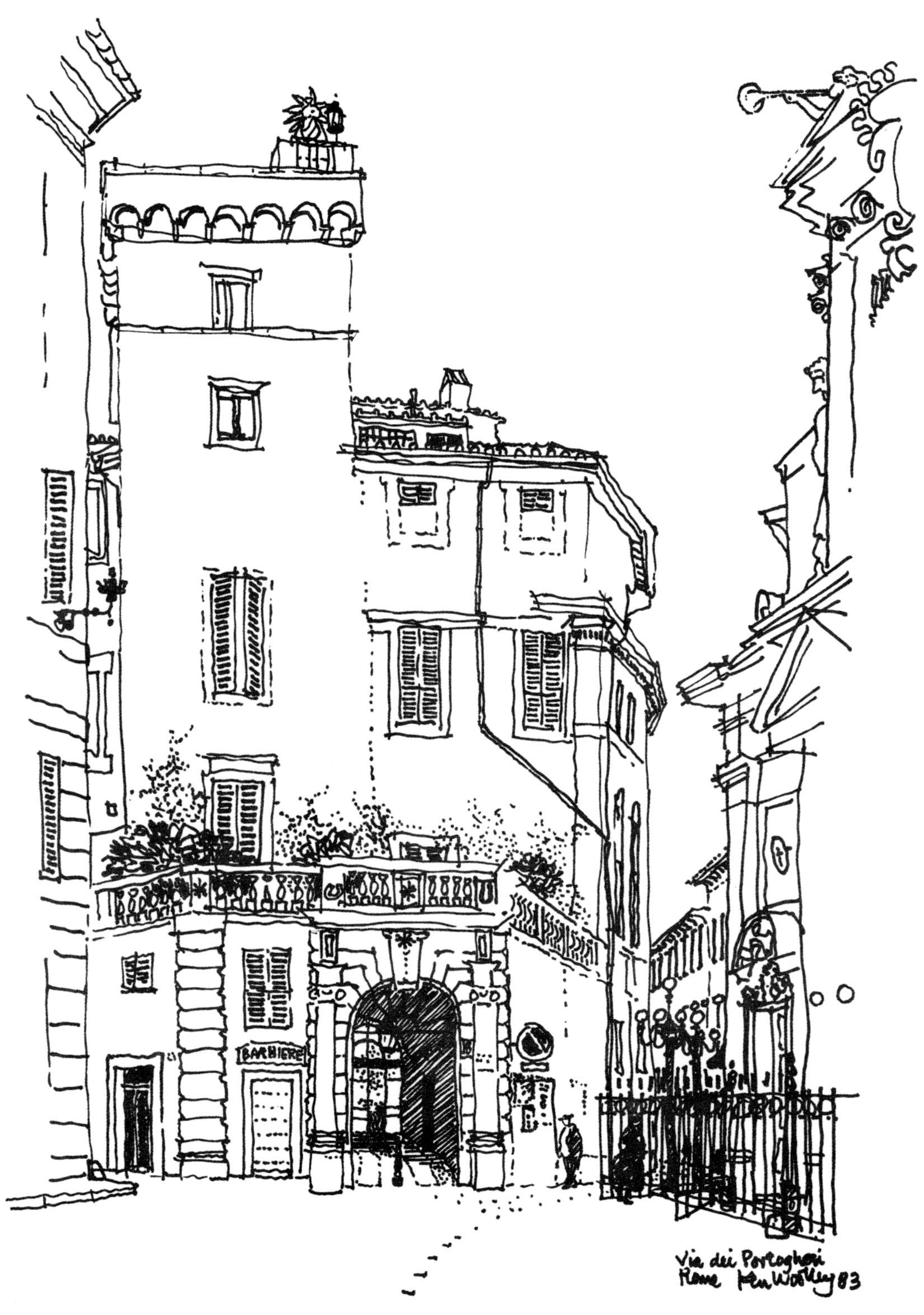

45

Via dei Portoghesi, Rome 1983

Pentel, cartridge paper 24 x 32.5

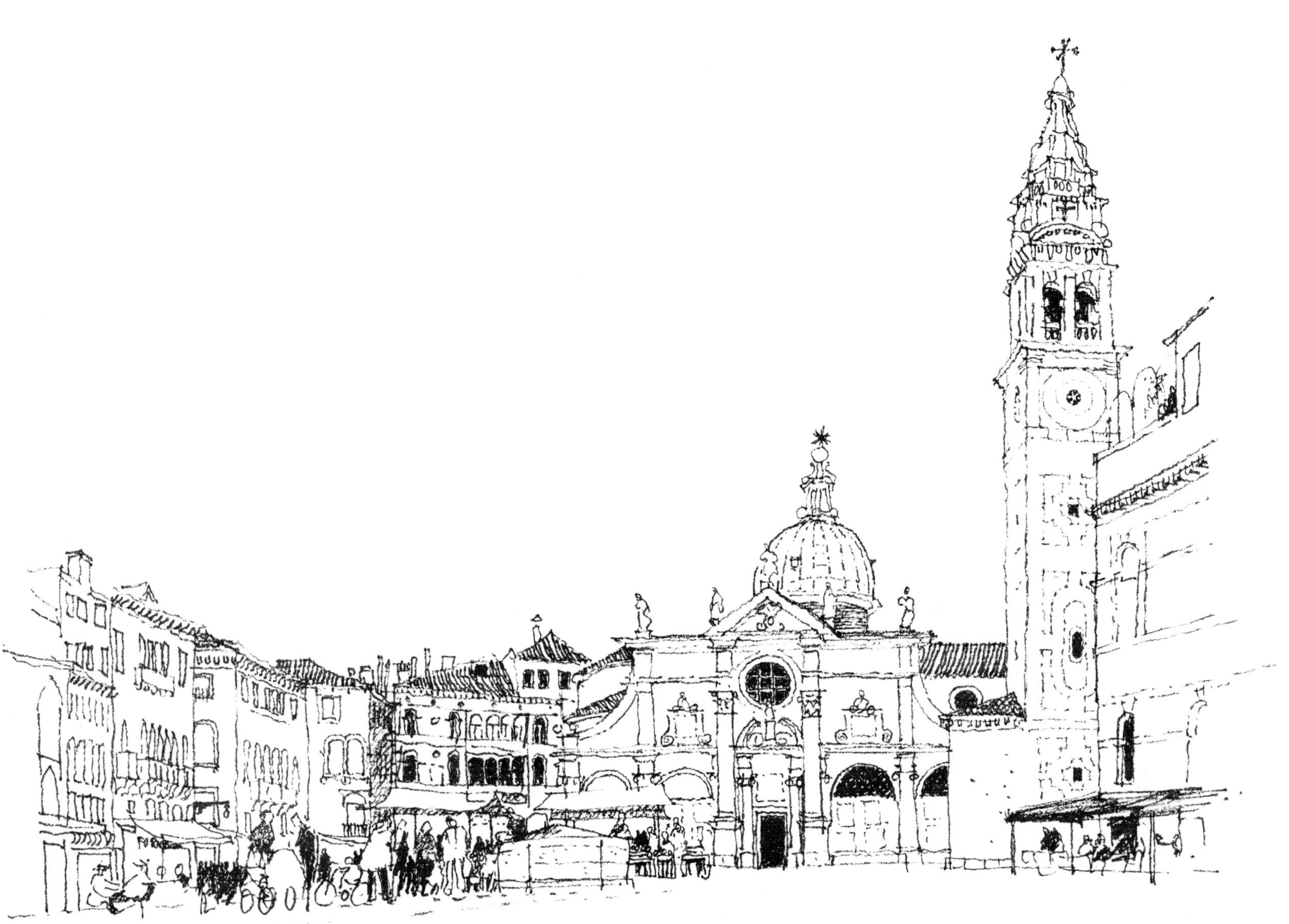

46

Campo S. Maria Formosa, Venice 1985

Pentel, Ingres paper 24 x 30.5 Exhibited

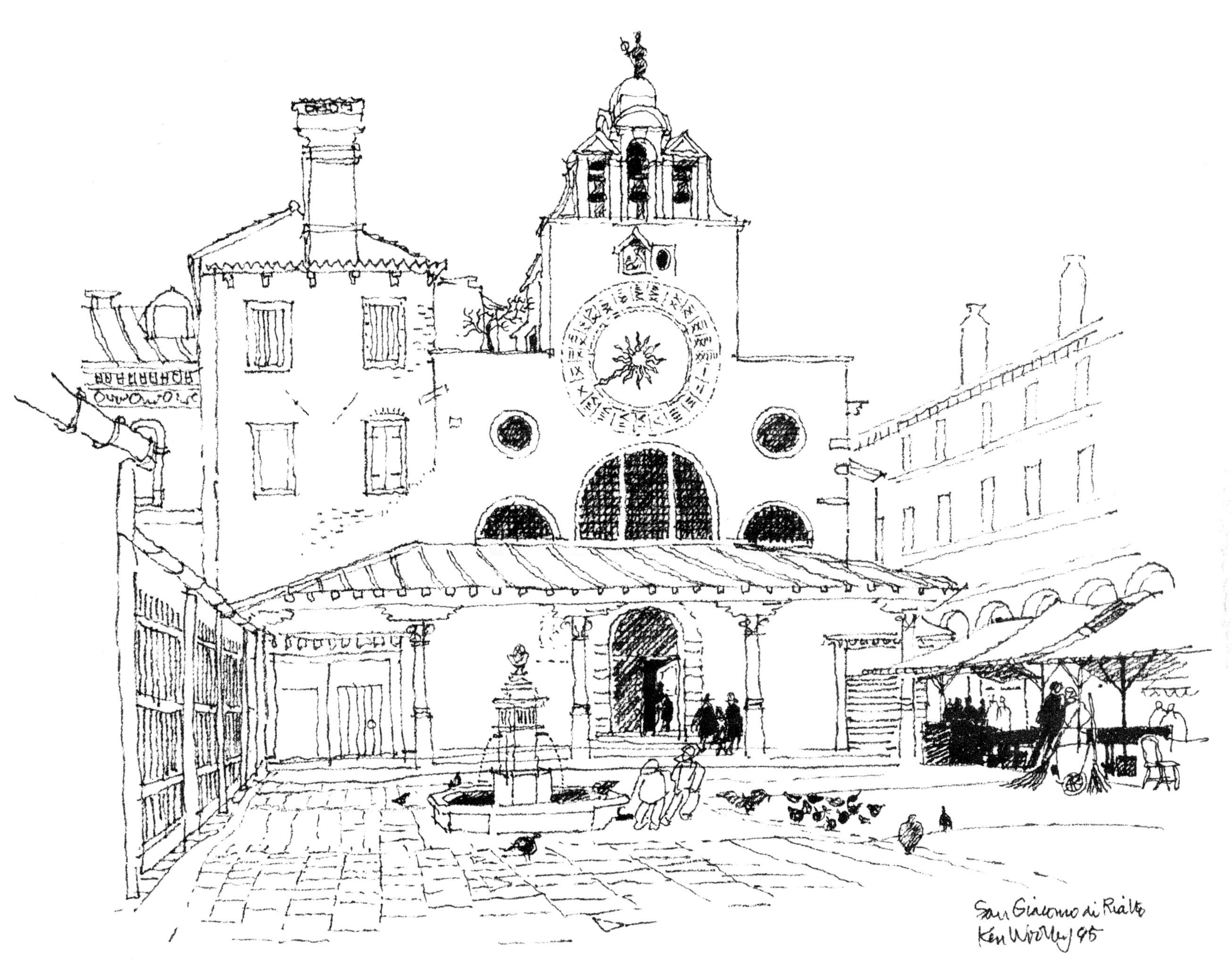

47
San Giacomo di Rialto, Venice 1985
Pentel, Ingres paper 24 x 30.5

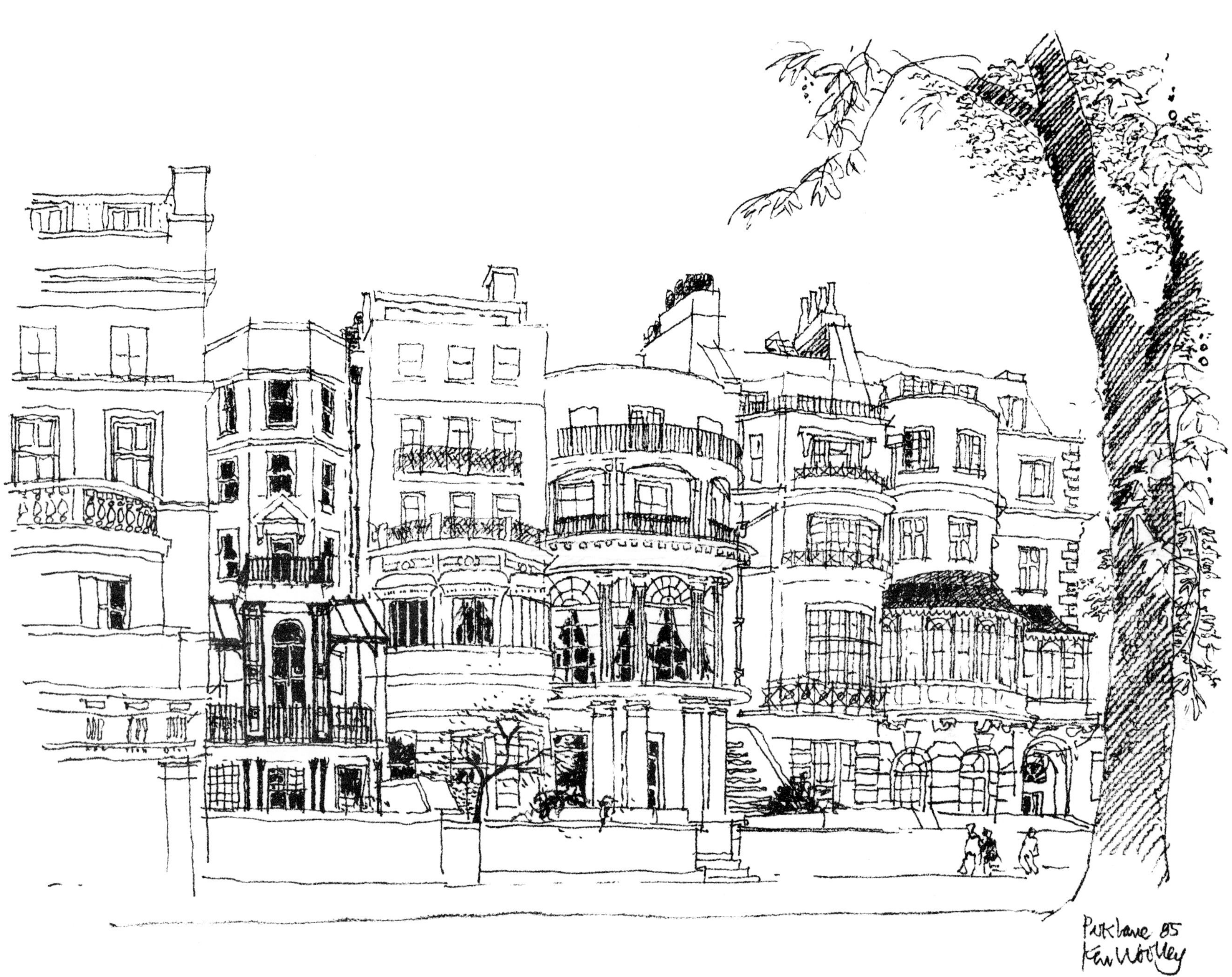

48

Park Lane, London 1985

Pentel, Ingres paper 24 x 32.5

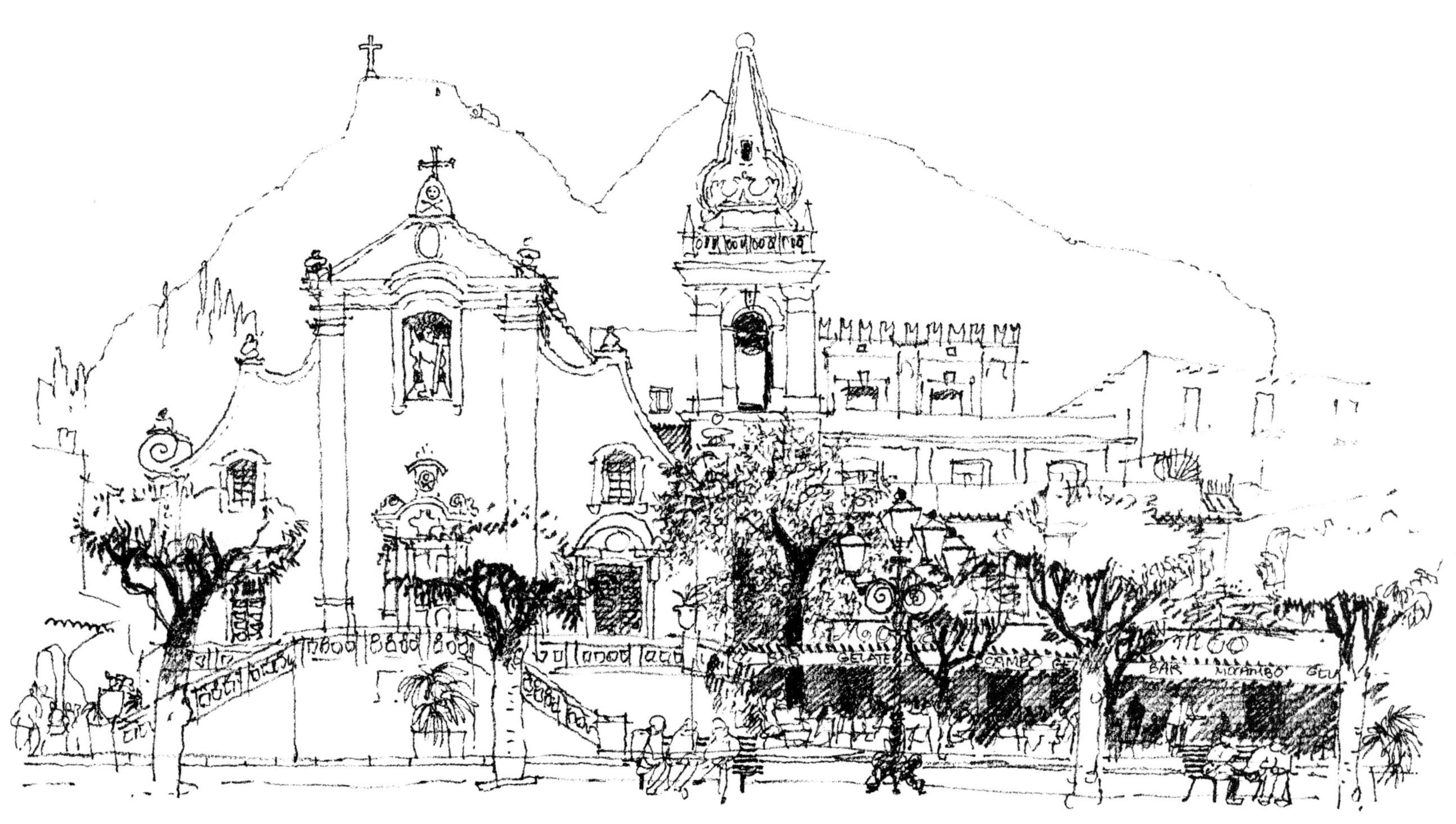

Taormina 87
Ken Woolley

49

Taormina, Sicily 1987

Pentel, Ingres paper 24 x 30.5 Exhibited

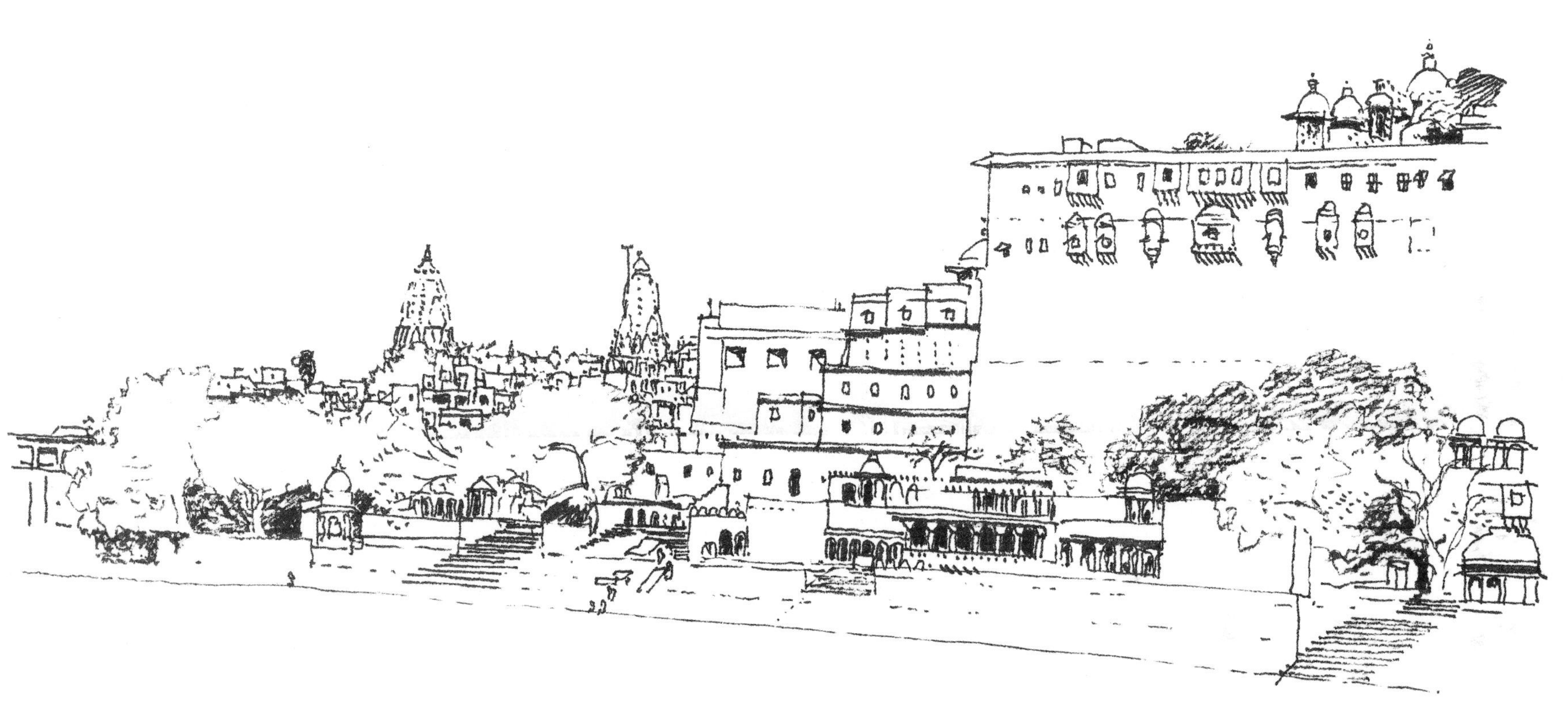

50

The Palace, old town and lake from the Floating Palace, Udaipur, India 1987

Pentel, Ingres paper 24 x 30.5 Exhibited

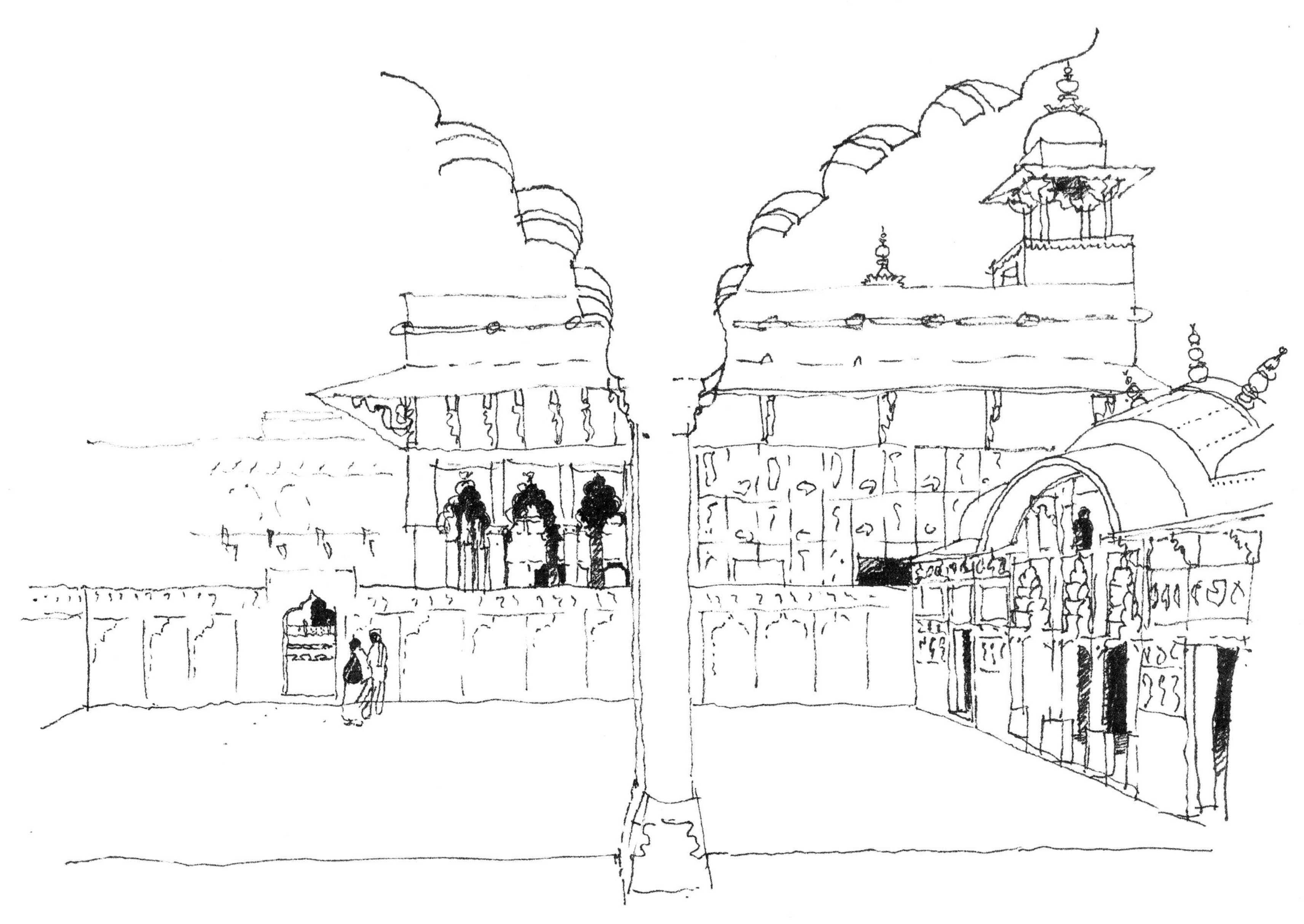

51

Courtyards in the Mogul Fort, Agra, India 1987

Pentel, Ingres paper 24 x 30.5 Exhibited

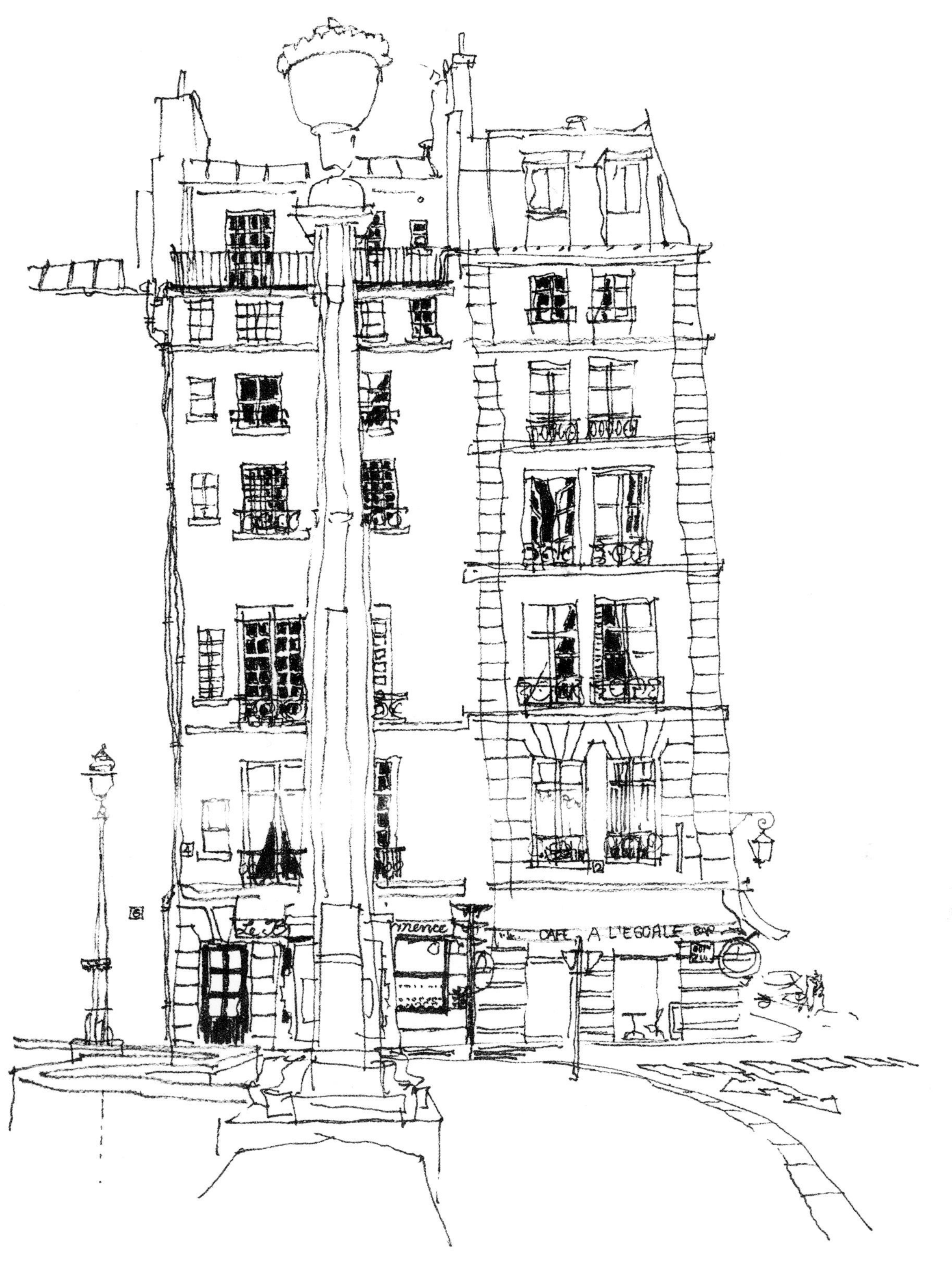

52

House on Isle S. Louis, second version, Paris 1989

Pentel, Ingres paper 24 x 30.5

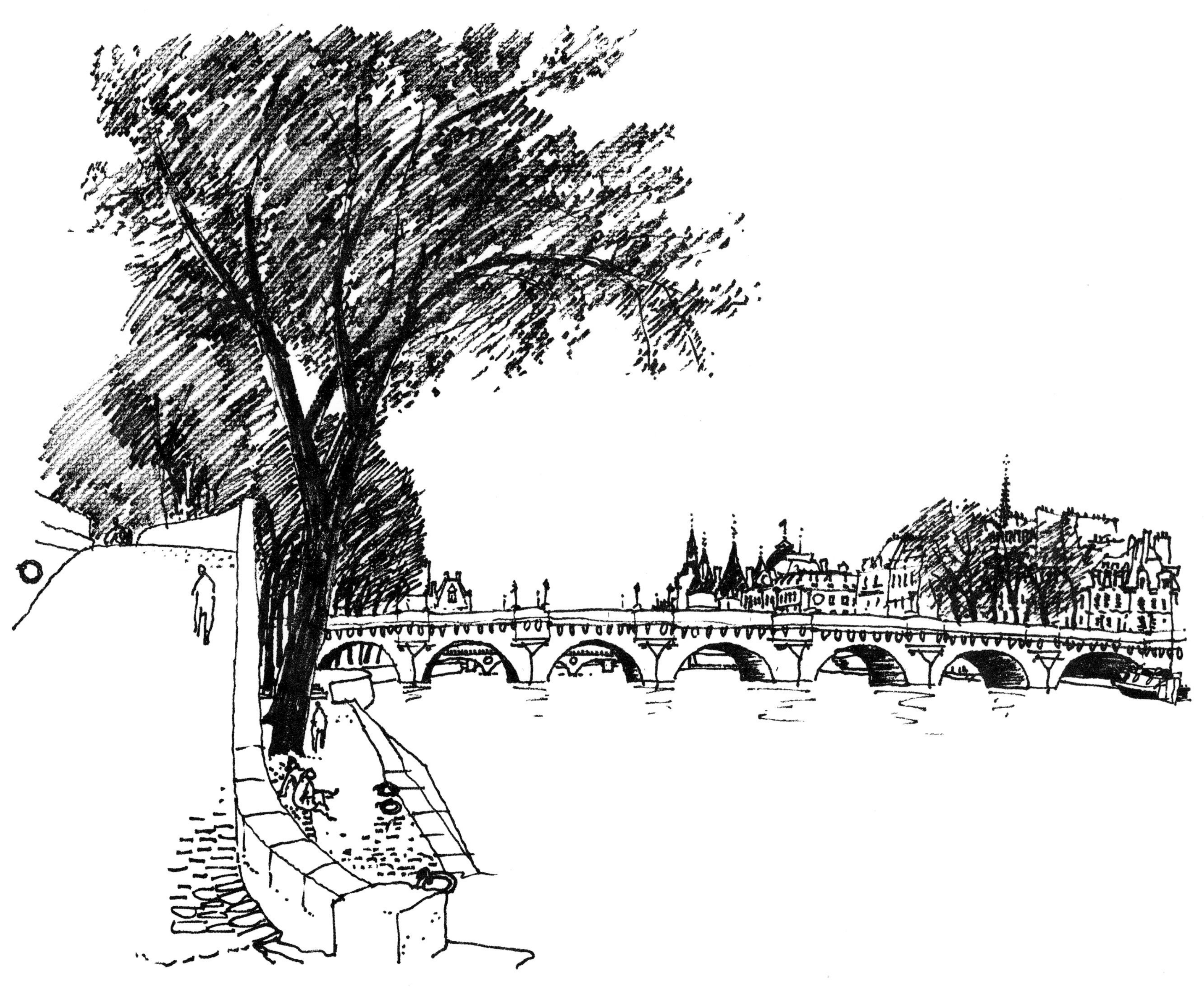

53
Seine embankment 33 years on, Paris 1989
Pentel, Ingres paper 23.5 x 29.5

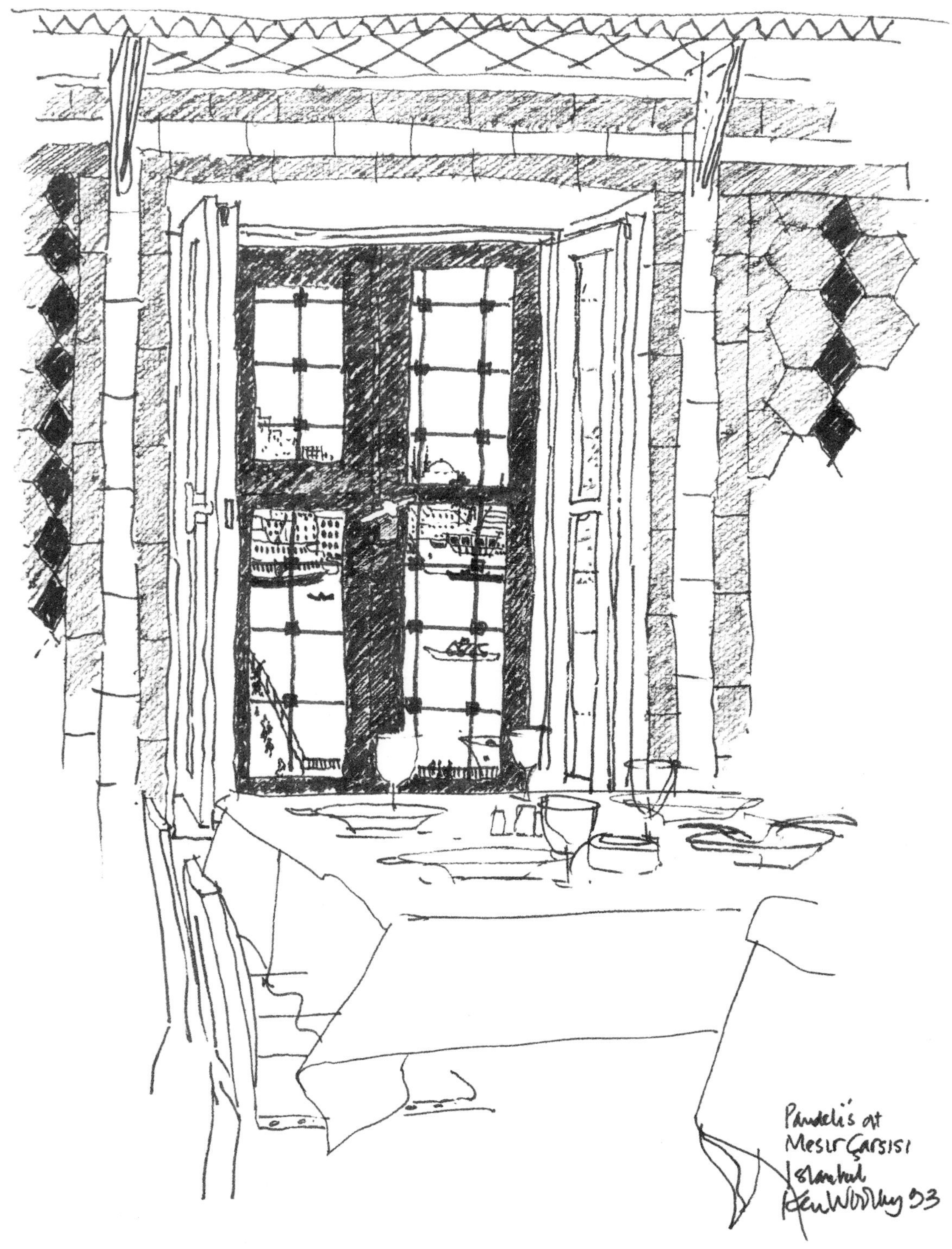

54

Pandeli's Restaurant at Mesir Carsisi, Istanbul 1993

Pentel, Ingres paper 23.5 x 29.5 Exhibited

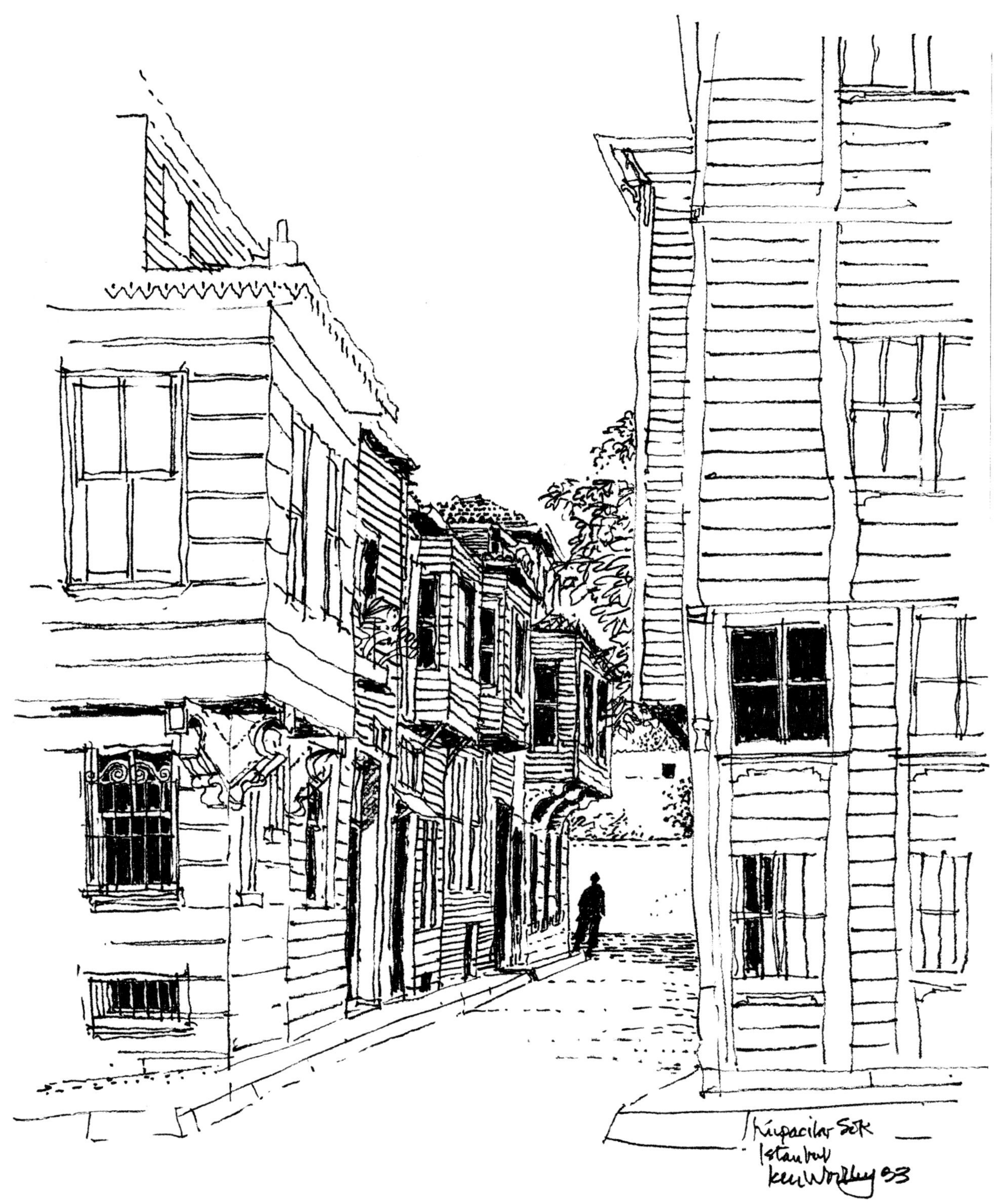

55
Timber houses, Istanbul 1993
Pentel, Ingres paper 23.5 x 29.5

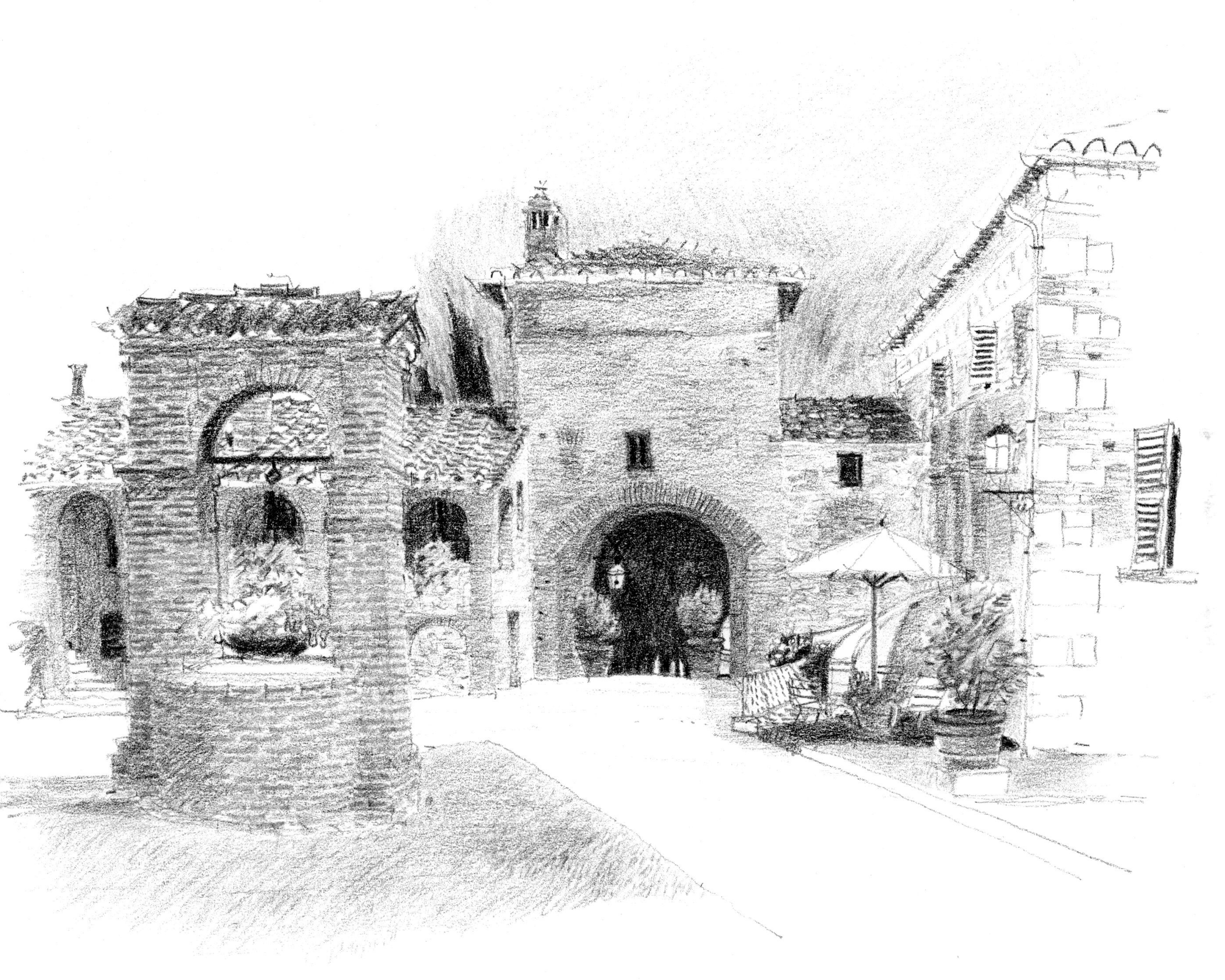

56

Fattoria del Amorosa, Tuscany 1993

Coloured pencil, cartridge paper 20 x 24.5 Exhibited

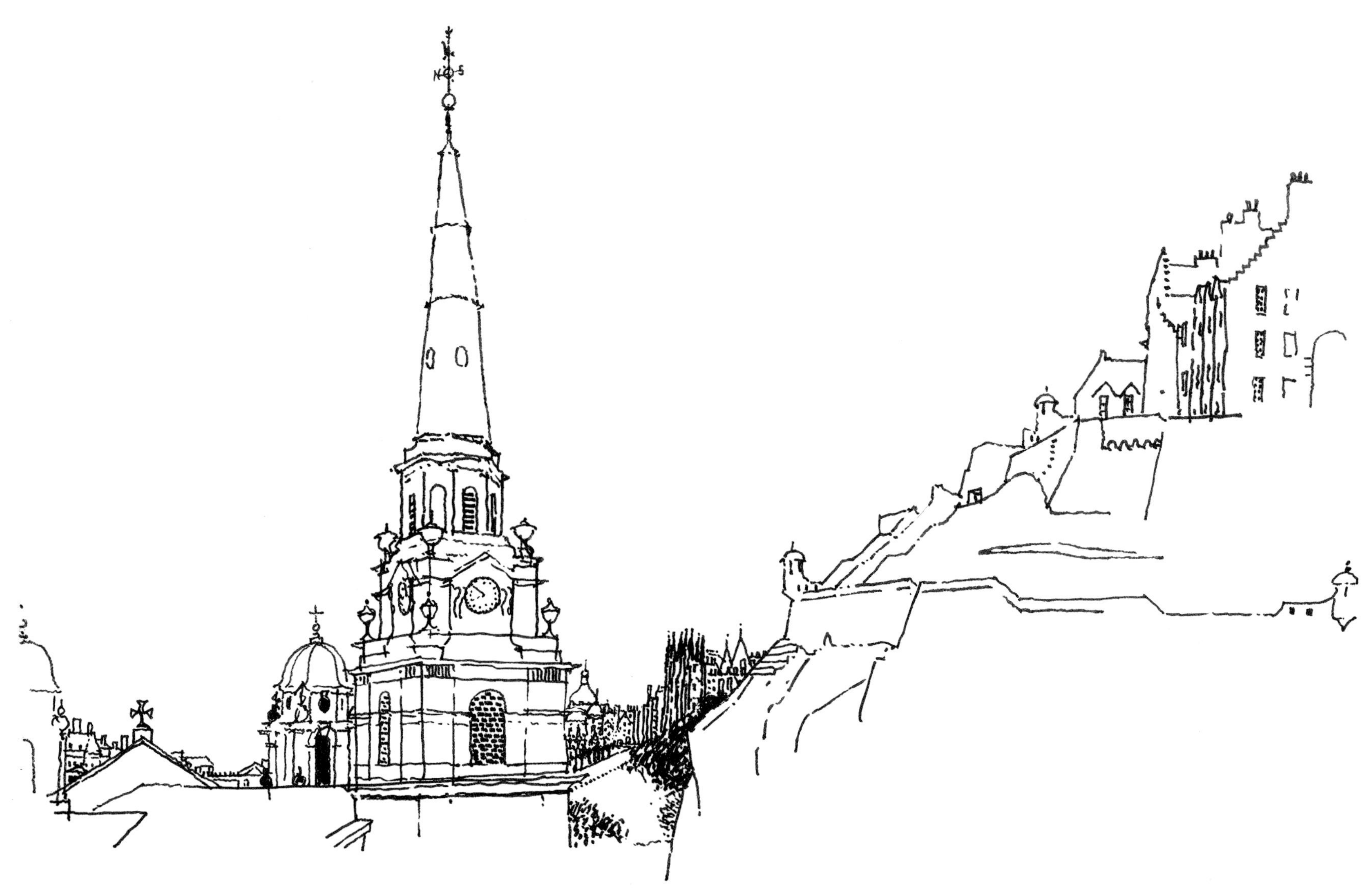

57

Edinburgh Castle, Scotland 1993

Pentel, Ingres paper 20 x 24.5

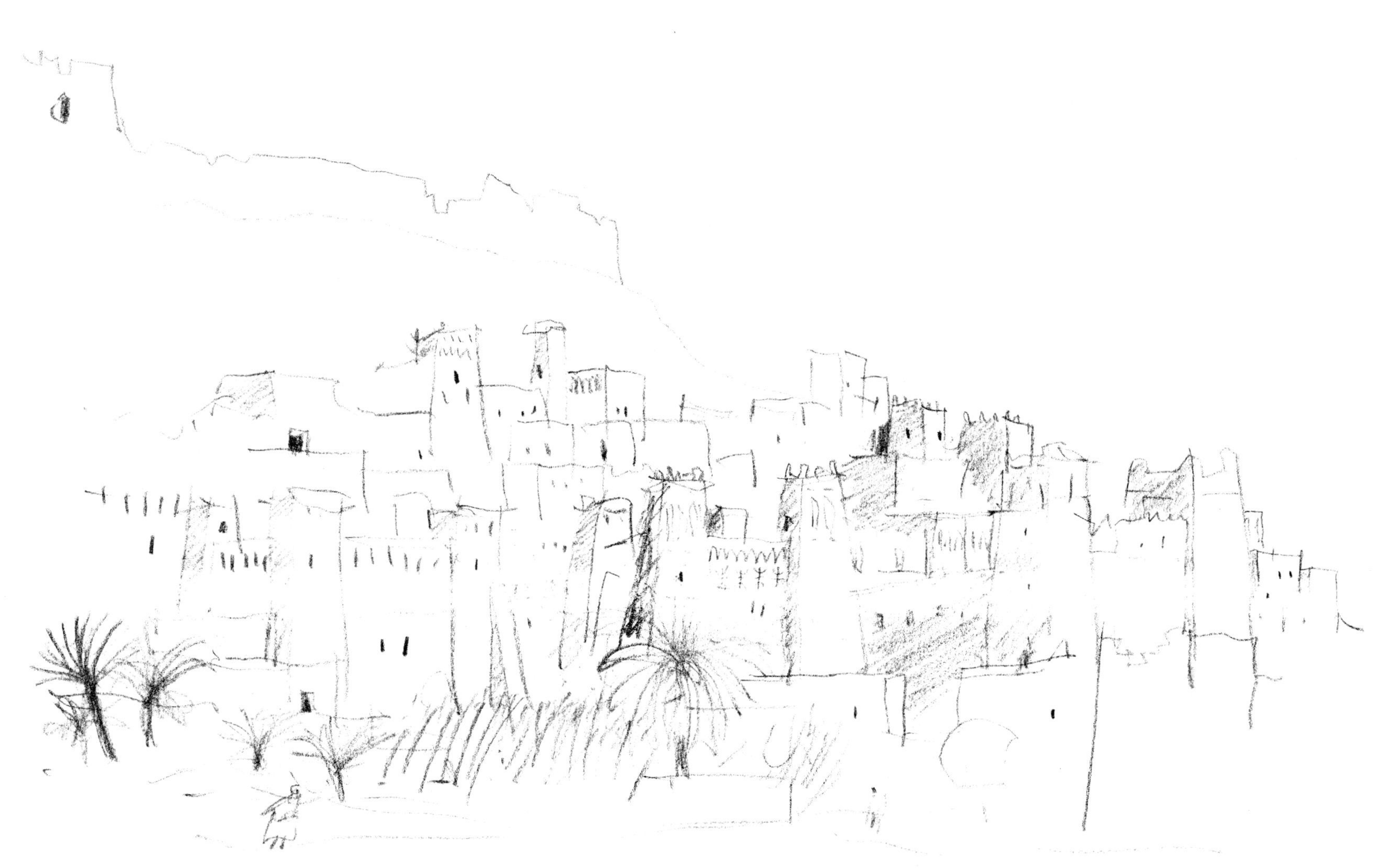

58

Abandoned Casbah, Ait-ben-Haddou, Morocco 1994

Pencil, cartridge paper 20 x 29.5

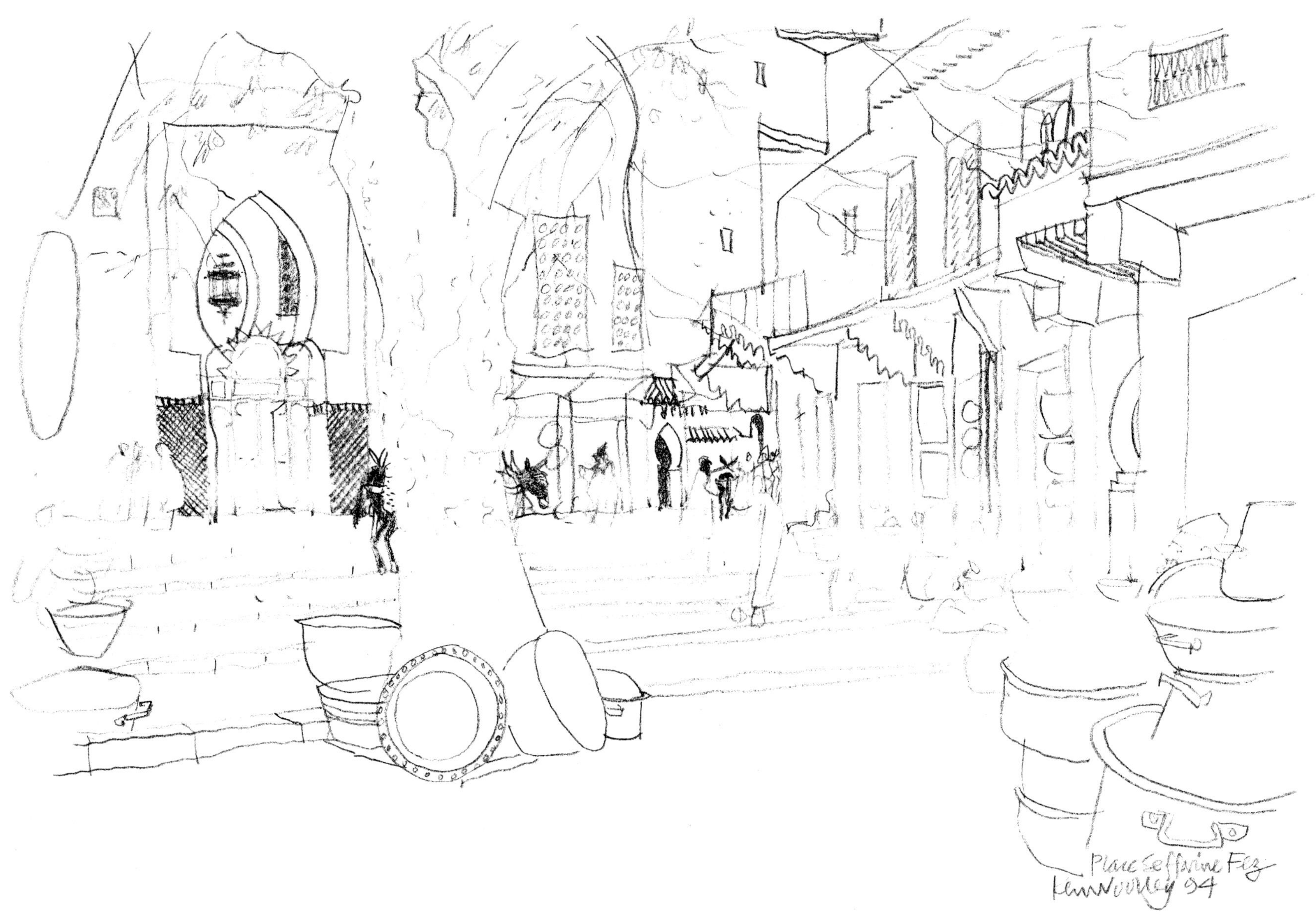

59

Place Seffarine, Fez, Morocco 1994

Pencil, cartridge paper 20 x 29.5 Exhibited

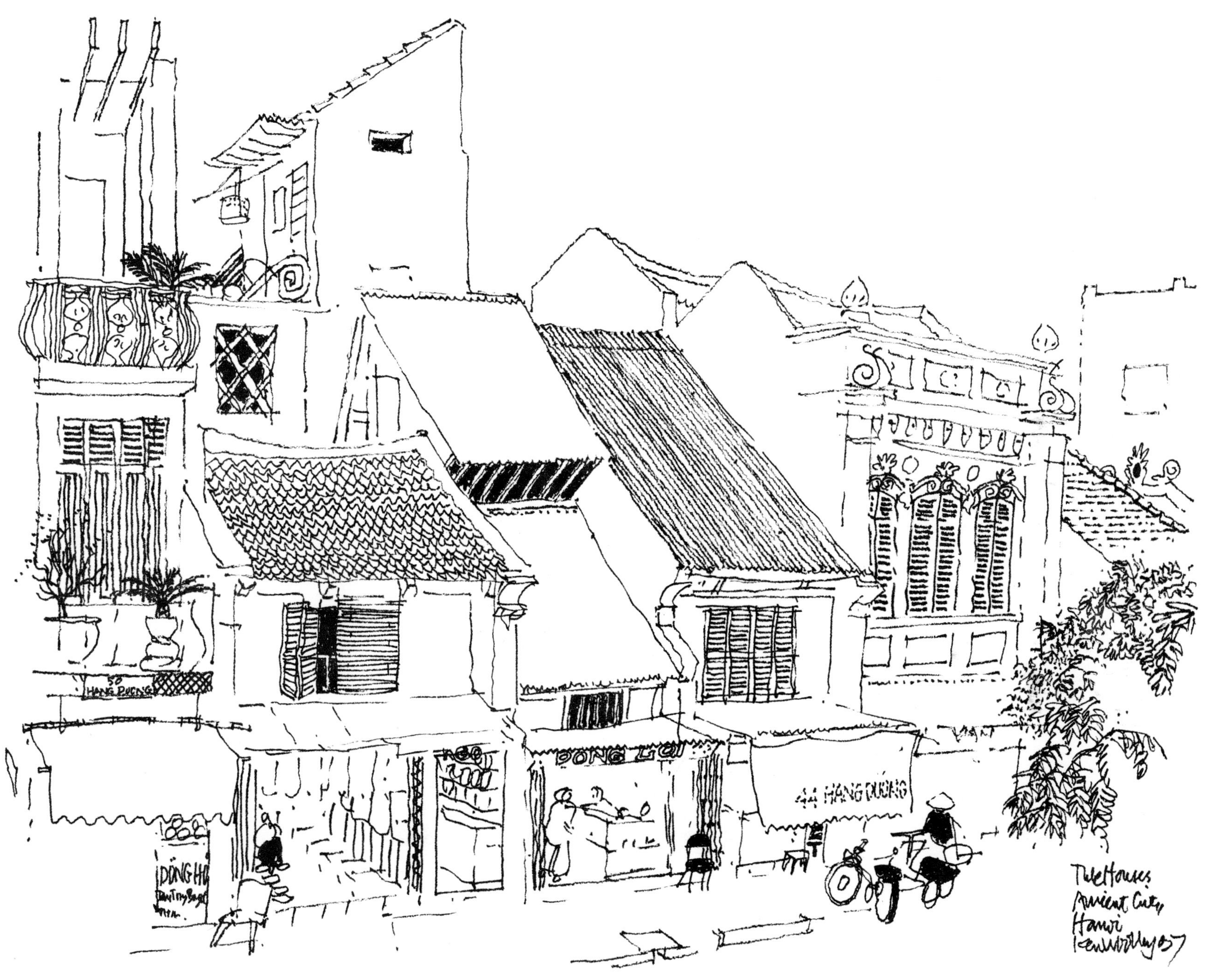

60

Tube houses, Ancient City, Hanoi, Vietnam 1997

Pentel, Ingres paper 23.5 x 29.5 Exhibited

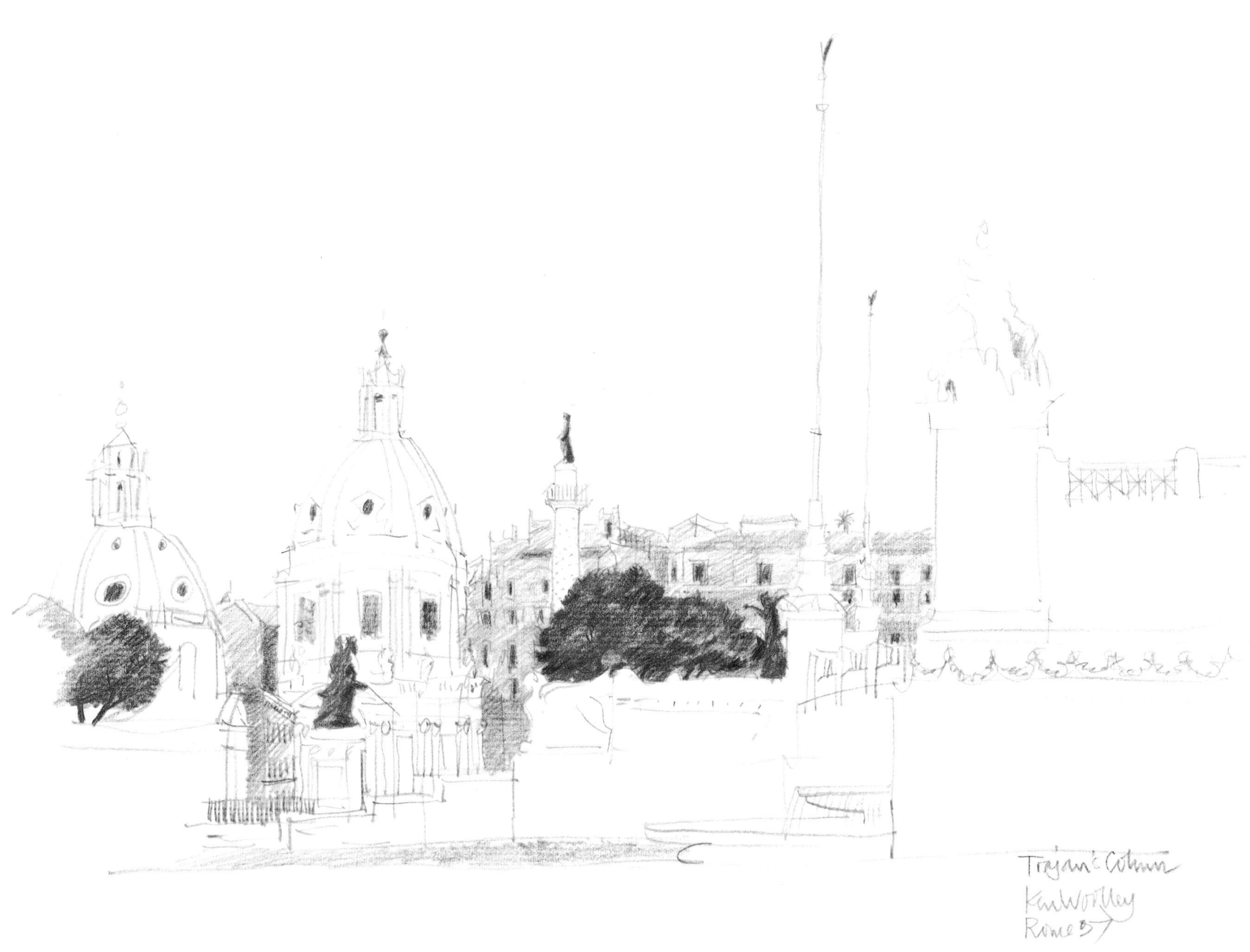

61

Trajan's Column and the Vittorio Emanuelle, Rome 1997

Carbon pencil, Ingres paper 23.5 x 32

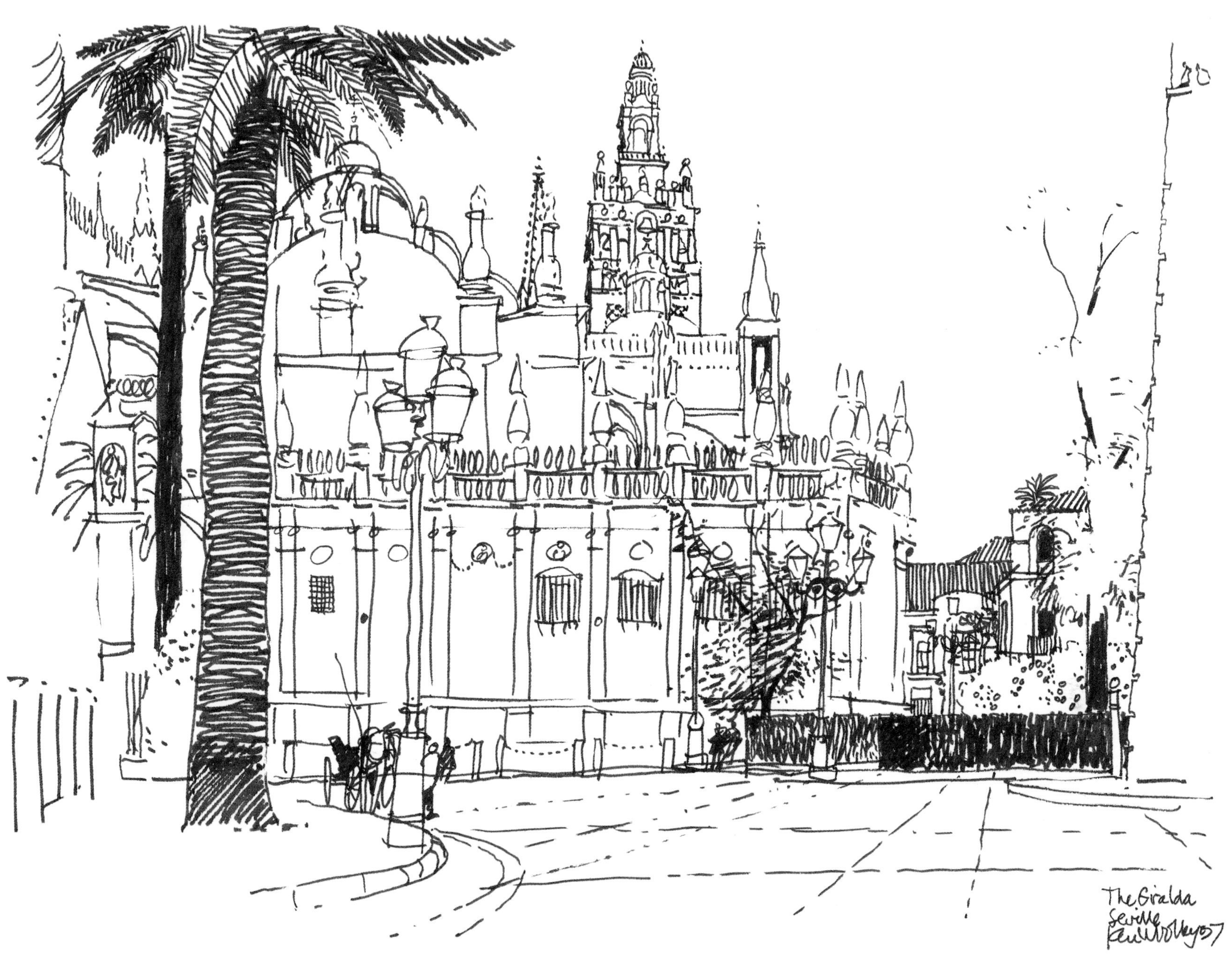

62
The Giralda, Seville 1997
Pentel, Ingres paper 23.5 x 32 Exhibited

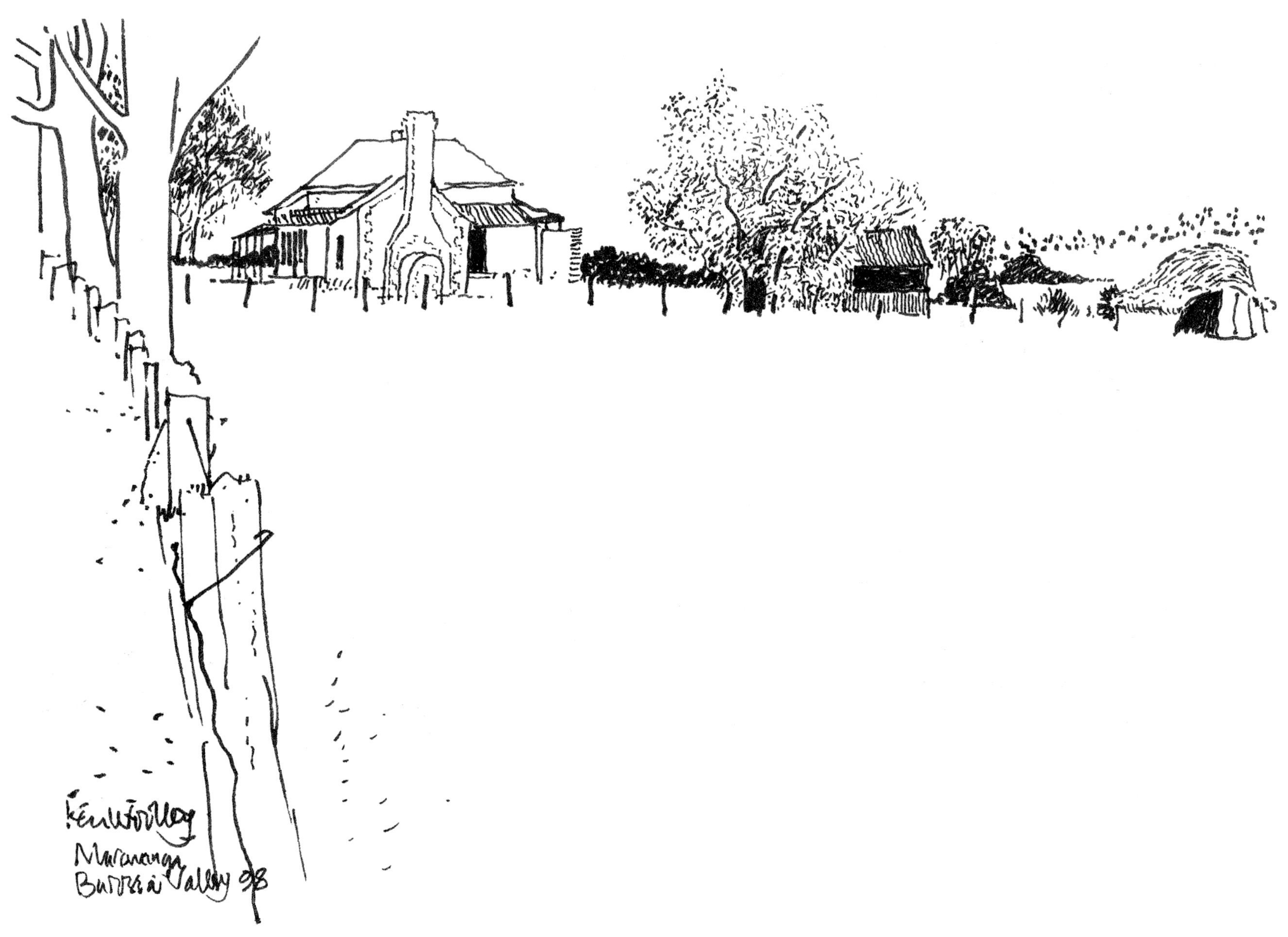

Marawanga, Barossa Valley, South Australia 1998
Pentel, cartridge paper 16 x 22

64

Poltalloch homestead, South Australia 1998

Carbon pencil, Ingres paper 24 x 32 Exhibited

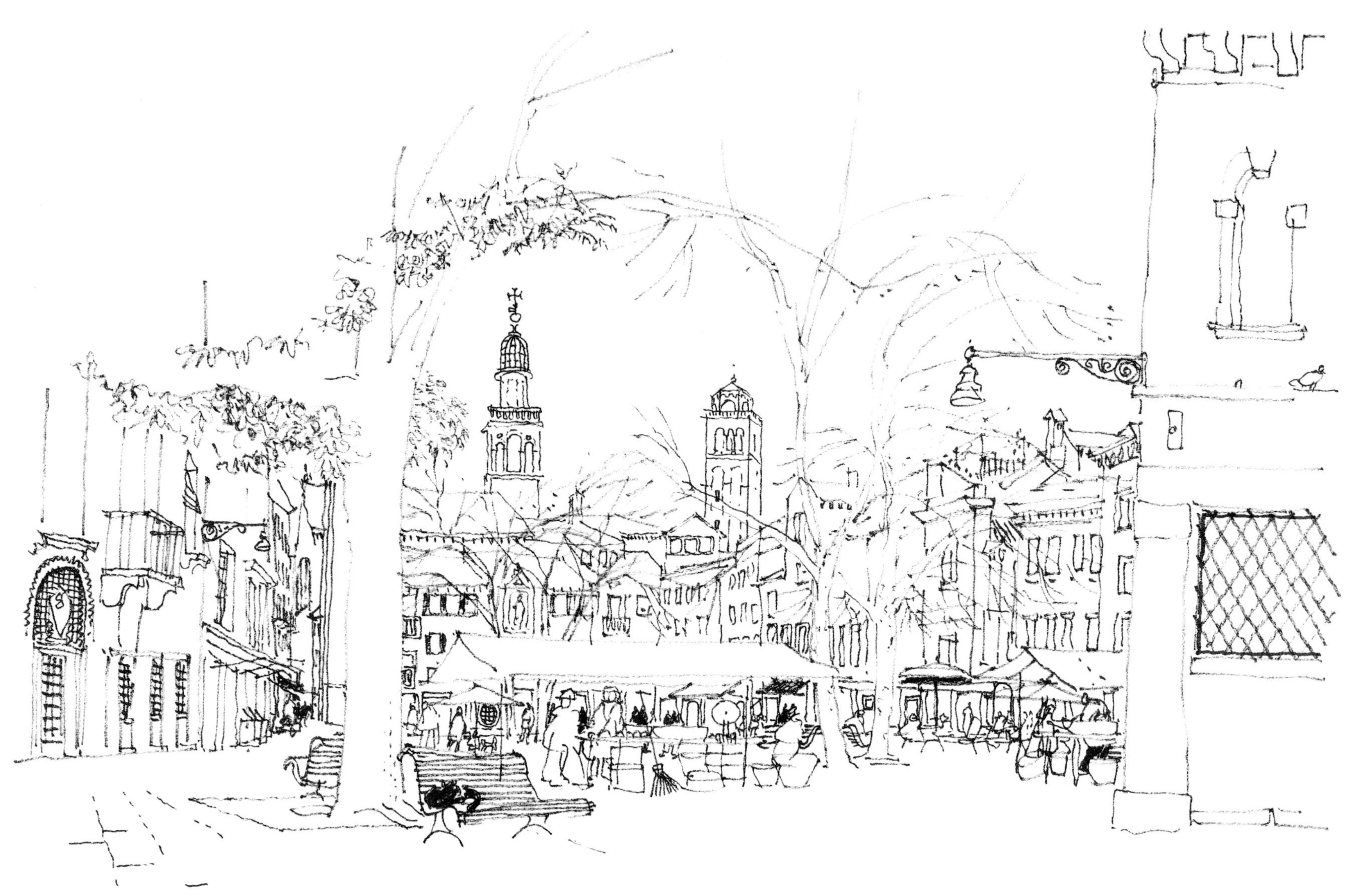

Campo S. Margherita Venice
Ken Woolley '99

65

Campo Santa Margherita, Venice 1999

Pentel, Ingres paper 24 x 32 Exhibited

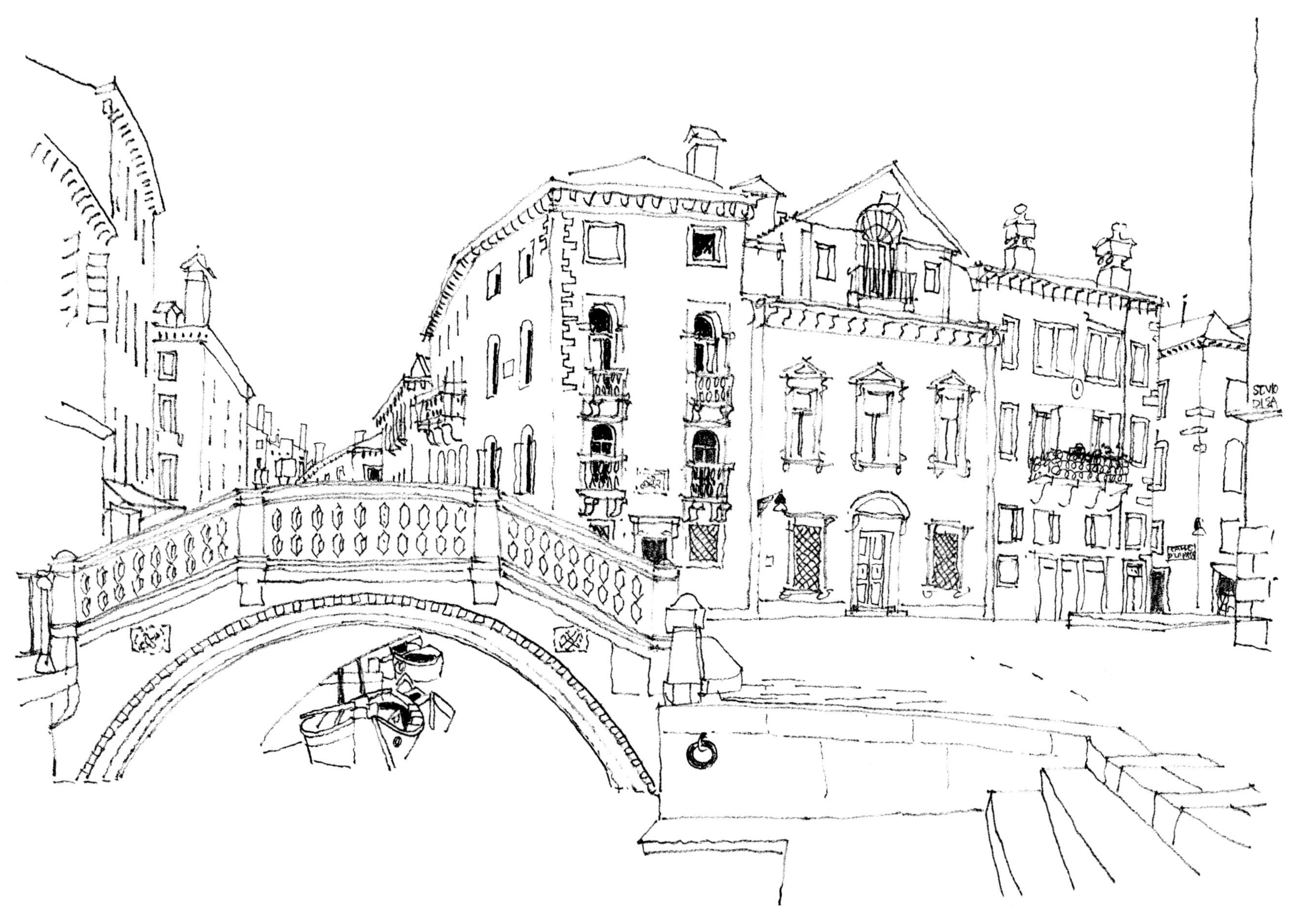

Campo dei Fiori, Venice 1999

Pentel, Ingres paper 24 x 32

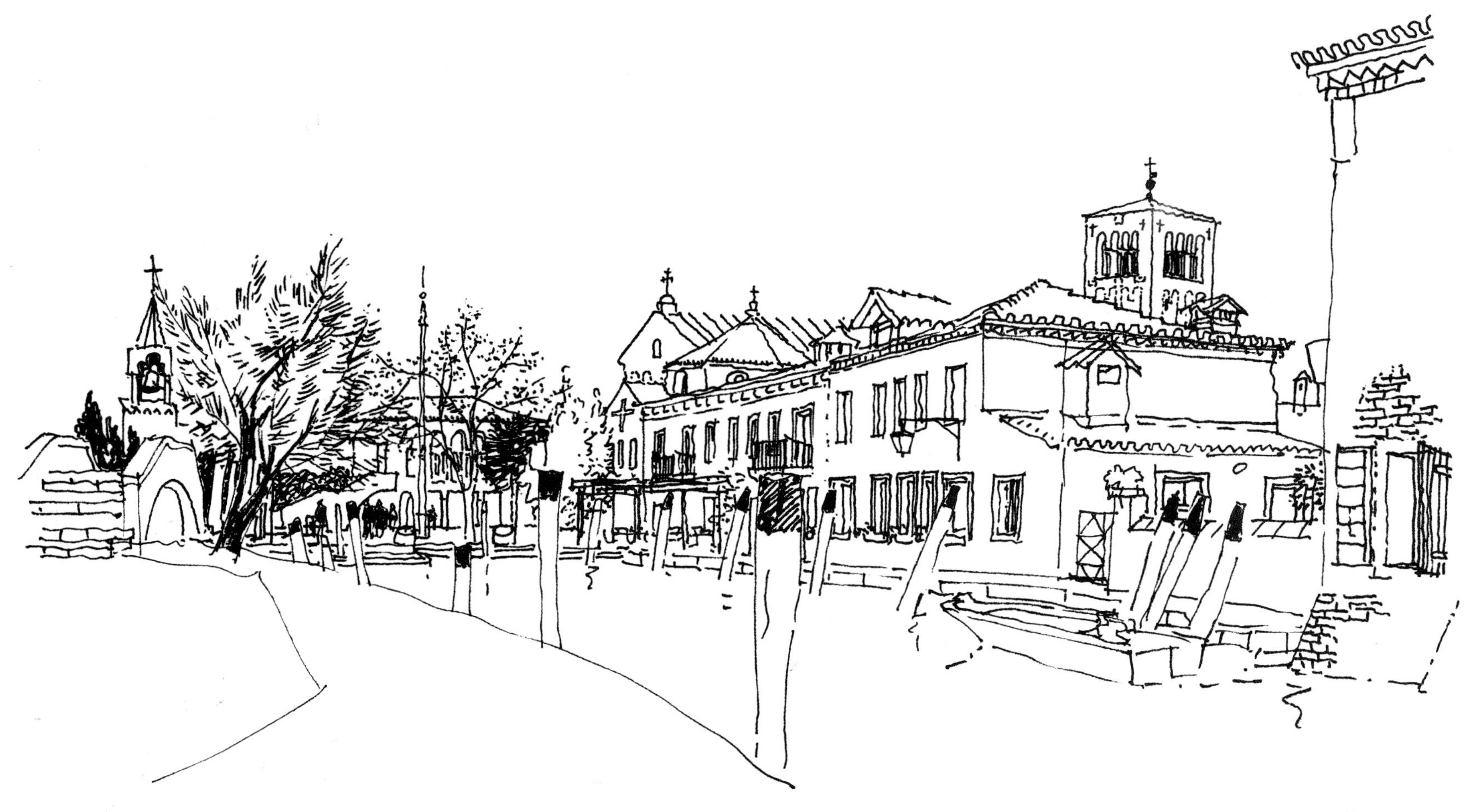

67

Torcello, Venice lagoon, Italy 1999

Pentel, cartridge paper 24 x 32

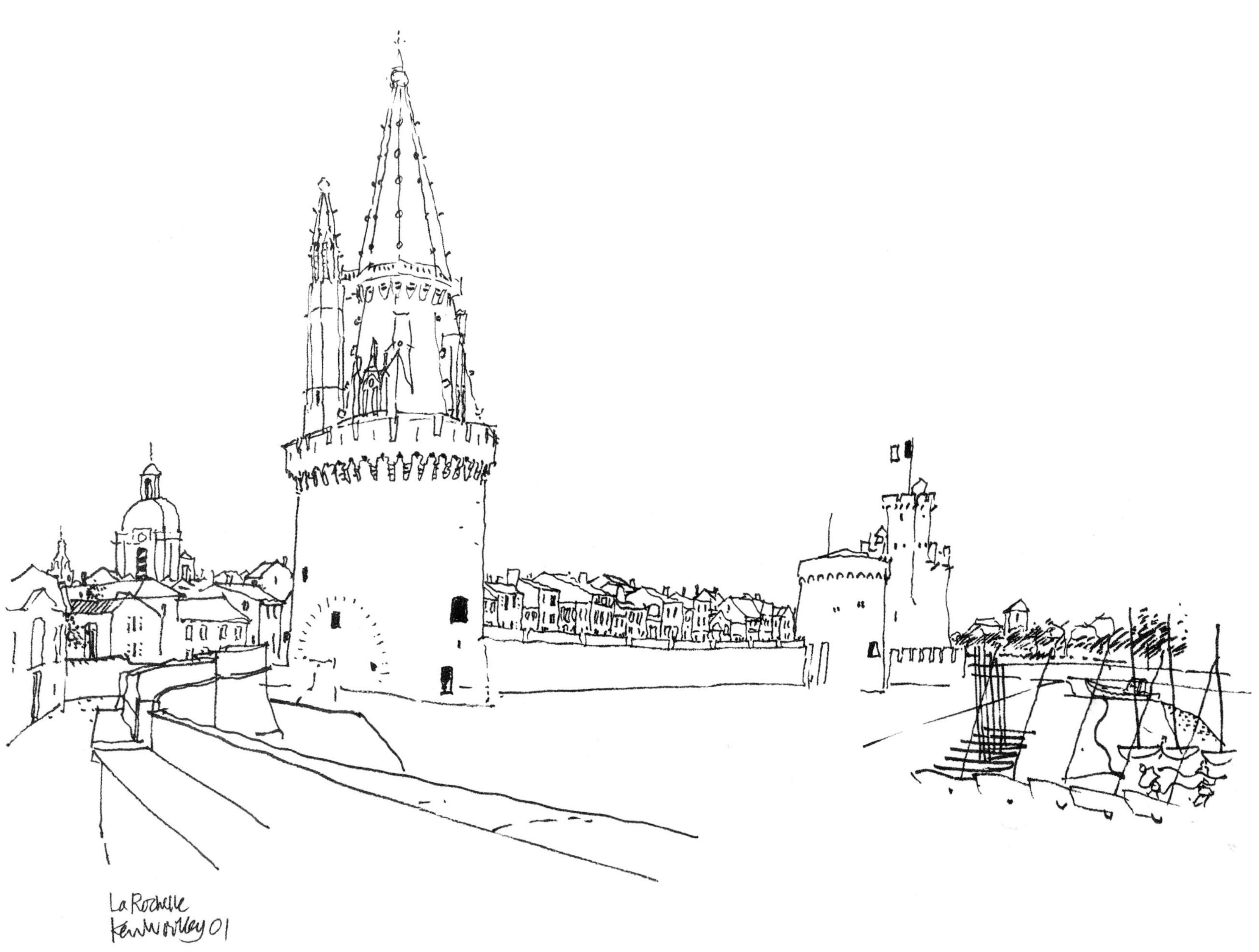

The Lantern Tower, La Rochelle, France 2001

Pentel, Ingres paper 24 x 32

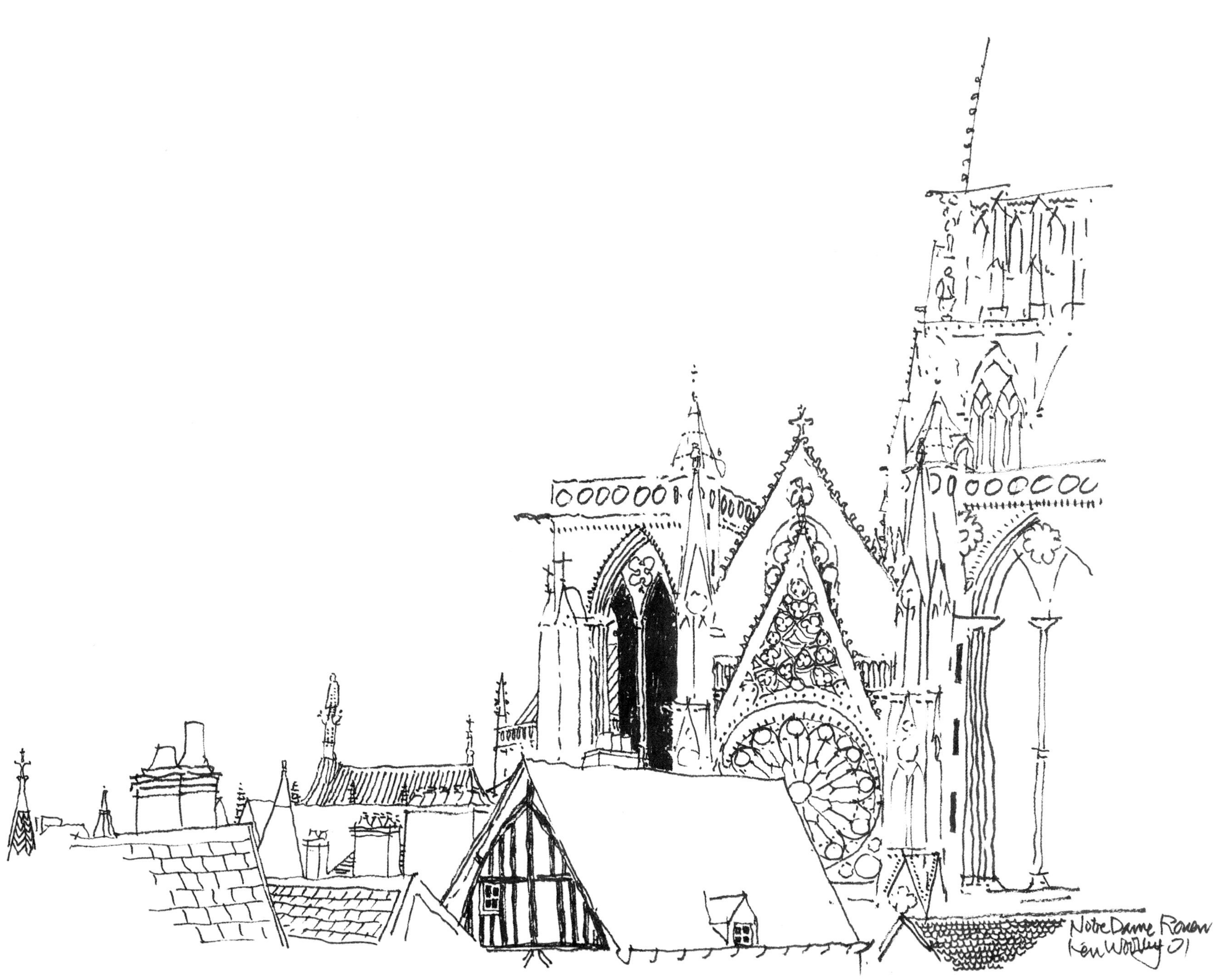

69

Notre Dame, Rouen, France 2001

Pentel, Ingres paper 24 x 32 Exhibited

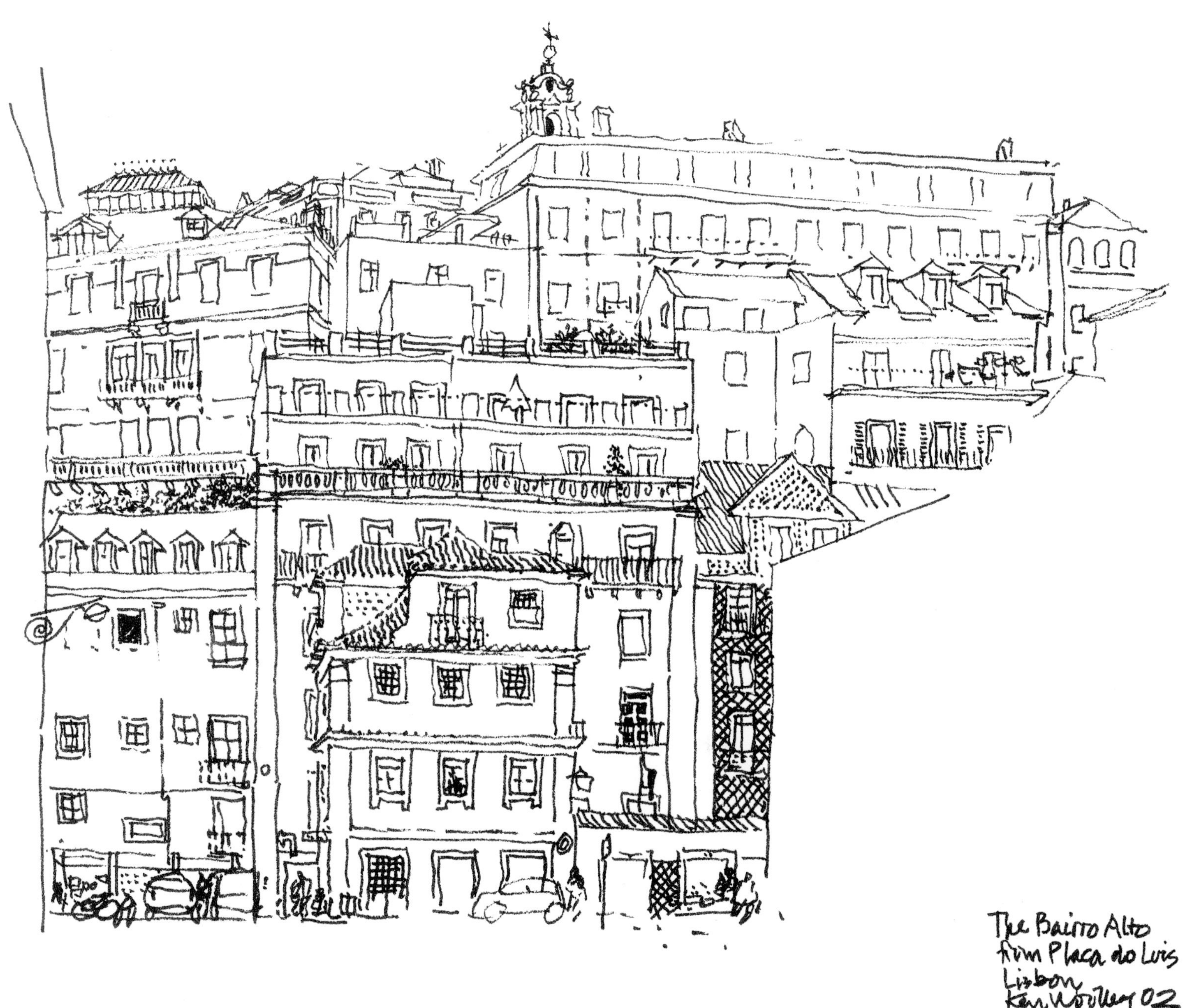

The Bairro Alto, Lisbon, Portugal 2002

Pentel, watercolour paper 18 x 24.5 Exhibited

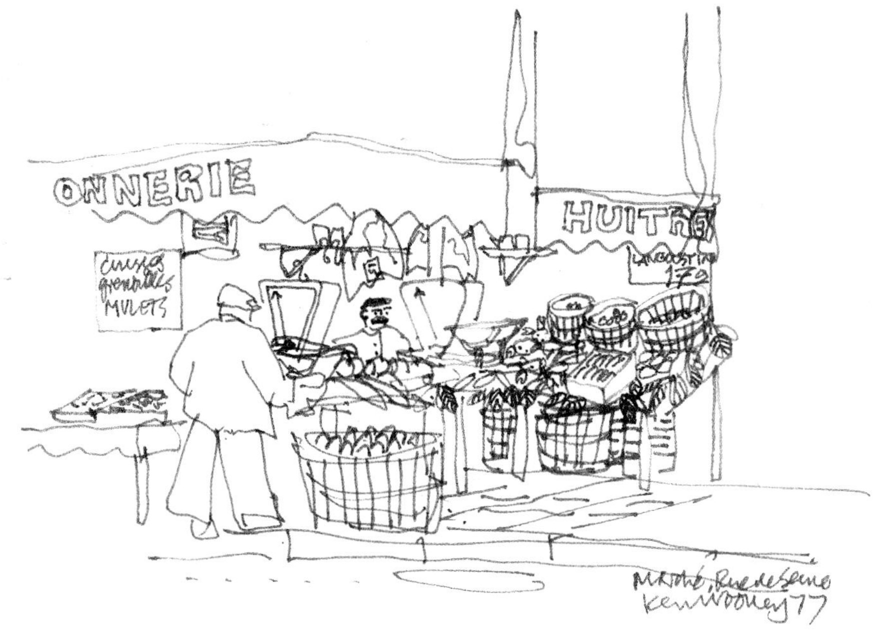

Market, Rue de Seine, Paris 1977

Pilot Fineliner, cartridge paper 9 x 12